Teach Yourself VISUALLY™
Pinterest™

Visual

Janet Majure

WILEY

John Wiley & Sons, Inc.

Teach Yourself VISUALLY™ Pinterest™

Published by
John Wiley & Sons, Inc.
10475 Crosspoint Boulevard
Indianapolis, IN 46256

www.wiley.com

Published simultaneously in Canada

Wiley publishes in a variety of print and electronic formats and by print-on-demand. Some material included with standard print versions of this book may not be included in e-books or in print-on-demand. If this book refers to media such as a CD or DVD that is not included in the version you purchased, you may download this material at http://booksupport.wiley.com. For more information about Wiley products, visit www.wiley.com.

Library of Congress Control Number: 2012948657

ISBN: 978-1-118-45907-2

Manufactured in the United States of America

10 9 8 7 6 5 4 3 2 1

Trademark Acknowledgments

Contact Us

For general information on our other products and services please contact our Customer Care Department within the U.S. at 877-762-2974, outside the U.S. at 317-572-3993 or fax 317-572-4002.

For technical support please visit www.wiley.com/techsupport.

WILEY **Sales** | Contact Wiley at (877) 762-2974 or fax (317) 572-4002.

Credits

Acquisitions Editor
Aaron Black

Project Editor
Jade L. Williams

Technical Editor
Donna Baker

Copy Editor
Lauren Kennedy

Editorial Director
Robyn Siesky

Business Manager
Amy Knies

Senior Marketing Manager
Sandy Smith

Vice President and Executive Group Publisher
Richard Swadley

Vice President and Executive Publisher
Barry Pruett

Project Coordinator
Katherine Crocker

Graphics and Production Specialists
Carrie A. Cesavice
Jill A. Proll

Quality Control Technician
Lindsay Amones

Proofreading
Melissa D. Buddendeck

Indexing
BIM Indexing & Proofreading Services

About the Author

Janet Majure is an author, writer, and editor with more than 30 years in the publishing industry. She writes or has written for three WordPress blogs (individual blogs Homecooking Revival.com and Foodperson.com plus group blog Ethicurean.com) and has written and edited books, newsletters, articles for daily newspapers, and technical white papers.

Author's Acknowledgments

The author gratefully acknowledges the longtime support and encouragement of friend, neighbor, colleague, and agent Neil Salkind. She also thanks Wiley editors Aaron Black and Jade Williams for their hard work getting this book into print.

How to Use This Book

Who This Book Is For

This book is for the reader who has never used this particular technology or software application. It is also for readers who want to expand their knowledge.

The Conventions in This Book

1 Steps

This book uses a step-by-step format to guide you easily through each task. **Numbered steps** are actions you must do; **bulleted steps** clarify a point, step, or optional feature; and **indented steps** give you the result.

2 Notes

Notes give additional information — special conditions that may occur during an operation, a situation that you want to avoid, or a cross-reference to a related area of the book.

3 Icons and Buttons

Icons and buttons show you exactly what you need to click to perform a step.

4 Tips

Tips offer additional information, including warnings and shortcuts.

5 Bold

Bold type shows command names or options that you must click or text or numbers you must type.

6 Italics

Italic type introduces and defines a new term.

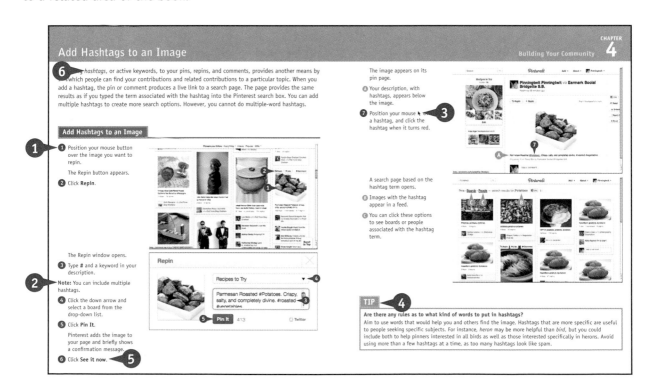

Table of Contents

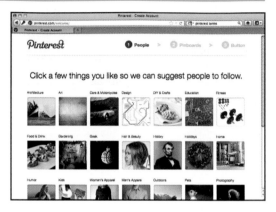

Chapter 3 | Refining Your Pinterest Setup

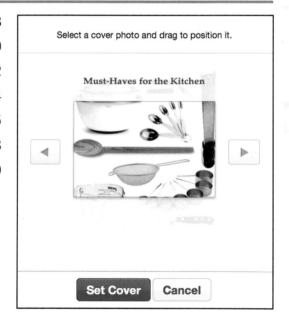

Table of Contents

Chapter 6　Expanding Your Pinning Options

Chapter 7　Promoting Your Business or Blog

Table of Contents

Chapter 10 Protecting Yourself

Chapter 11 Getting Help

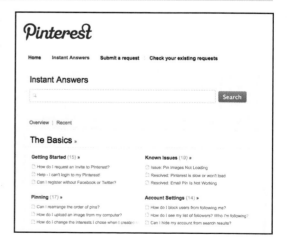

CHAPTER 1

Getting Started with Pinterest

Viewing images at Pinterest is fun, but when you sign up to become a Pinterest member, you will be able to view, collect, organize, rate, and comment on images at http://pinterest.com. Getting started may well be the hardest thing about Pinterest, if only because you have so many ways to join. Once you are in, the fun really begins.

Introducing Pinterest

You can organize your plans, your wish lists, your collections — almost anything that you might organize through images — by using Pinterest. One picture is worth a thousand words, after all, and Pinterest lets you take advantage of that principle by offering *virtual pinboards* on which you can post the images that interest, inspire, or otherwise help you. As you become more familiar with Pinterest, you will see how it works toward the site's goal of connecting people through their common interests.

How Pinterest Works

Anyone can look at the pictures on Pinterest, but when you join as a member, you can save and organize your favorite images to your personal virtual pinboards. You also can write comments on images that you or other people post, and you can register which pictures you like, even when you do not want to save the pictures for yourself. In addition, as a Pinterest member, you can follow the activity of particular Pinterest users or specific pinboards that other Pinterest users maintain. You can even share a pinboard with other members.

Wash Cloths

Why Join Pinterest?

With the seemingly endless array of social networks and photo-sharing sites on the web, you may wonder why you would want another. You probably will like Pinterest for the same reasons it has become enormously popular: Pinterest is simple and fun and enables you to share and organize images more easily and beautifully than any other site. Many users also like the overall positive tone of Pinterest, and they like the idea of connecting with people who share their interests — whether they are recipes or fast cars — rather than keeping up with the daily drama in other people's lives.

Get Started with Pinterest

The first step in getting familiar with Pinterest is to type **http://pinterest.com** into your web browser's address bar and then scroll through the Pinterest home page. You will see an endless array of images, most with brief captions, and many with comments following them. When you see an image that interests you, click it. The image will open in its own window. There, Pinterest reveals more comments, shows the source of the image, and presents buttons that make it easy to reuse the image, known as a *pin*. Some of those options are even available when you are not a member.

Guacamole Bruschetta

486 likes   10 comments   4208 repins

What Shows Up on Pinterest

The most popular categories on Pinterest involve home decorating, cooking, clothing, and crafts. Still, you will find 32 categories, including the catch-all Other category. You are sure to find idea-filled images in whatever area might interest you. Sometimes the images essentially are pictures of words, so you can even find funny or inspirational quotes. The categories, meanwhile, are just one means of finding items. Pinterest offers multiple ways to search, and some participants, known as *pinners*, add key terms specifically to aid in searches. In short, if you are interested in something, you probably will find images related to it on Pinterest.

Pinterest

Everything ▾ · Videos · Popular · Gifts ▾

Architecture	Kids
Art	My Life
Cars & Motorcycles	Women's Apparel
Design	Men's Apparel
DIY & Crafts	Outdoors
Education	People
Film, Music & Books	Pets
Fitness	Photography
Food & Drink	Print & Posters

Discover Things You Love

Using Pinterest lets you discover images that interest you without requiring you to search for them specifically. Pinterest shows you images that individuals like you have posted because they are enthusiastic about the pictures or ideas they present. You can discover images that may excite you by viewing a cascade of images that are in a particular category or that are especially popular. You also can watch what individuals who share your tastes are posting, or *pinning*, on Pinterest. In contrast, search engines, such as the Google image search, require a specific search term and then present images without context.

Get Organized

Once you join, you can start pinning your favorite things, and you can organize them in ways that are useful to you. If you like to cook, you can create collections of images, called *boards*, of healthy recipes, special occasion main dishes, and favorite desserts. If you own a business, you might create boards for holiday products or how-to images. If you are planning a wedding, you can create boards for wedding dresses, invitations, flower arrangements, reception ideas, and honeymoon destinations.

guitar
53 likes 16 repins

Ron Alton The guitar of my dreams!

Chet Farnam Where did you find this?! I've looked everywhere!!!

Join Pinterest Using Your E-mail Address

Y ou can keep your Pinterest account independent from your other social networks when you join Pinterest by using your e-mail address. Joining by e-mail is a simple process. You simply pick a unique user name, provide your name and e-mail address, and then you are a member in moments. If you later decide you want to tie in your Pinterest activity with your Facebook or Twitter accounts, you can simply add that information. The first step, though, is to sign up.

Join Pinterest Using Your E-mail Address

1 In your internet browser, go to **http://pinterest.com/ join/signup**.

2 Click your email address.

The screen changes.

3 Type a username.

4 Type your e-mail address.

5 Type a password.

6 Type your first name.

7 Type your last name.

8 Click **Create Account**.

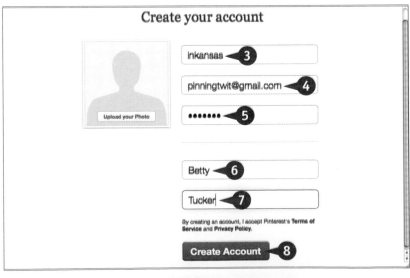

The Welcome page appears.

9 Click an image that you like.

A A thumbnail of the image appears.

10 Repeat Step **9** until you have clicked five images that interest you.

11 Click **Continue**.

B The Pinterest home page opens with a note asking you to verify your e-mail address.

12 Go to your e-mail account, open the e-mail message from Pinterest, and click **Verify Email**.

Your browser opens to the Pinterest home page, with you logged in.

Note: For more information on completing your sign-up, see the "Complete Your Sign-Up" section in this chapter.

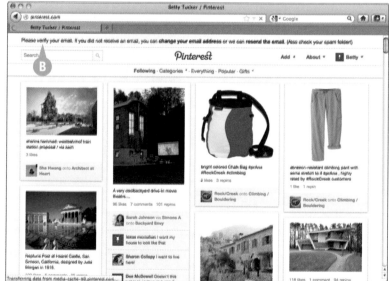

Will my name appear publicly?
Yes. Your username is for logging in and becomes part of the URL for your Pinterest page, but your name as entered in the First Name and Last Name boxes appears with every item you pin and every comment you make. However, there is nothing preventing you from using a pseudonym.

Why did I receive a 502-error message after I clicked Continue and choose my username?
It is not your fault. Most likely, you received the message because of Pinterest server problems. Try again in a little while, and it probably will be fine.

Join Pinterest Using Facebook

You can join Pinterest by using your current Facebook account. This medium enables you to complete your Pinterest sign-up after you receive an invitation to join. Besides making the process easy, using an existing Facebook account later makes signing in to Pinterest easy and allows you to share your Pinterest activity on your Facebook timeline. If you want to use Facebook but do not have a Facebook account, you will need to sign up with Facebook.

Join Pinterest Using Facebook

1 In the Facebook Login window, type your e-mail address.

A If you do not have a Facebook account, click **Sign Up** instead of typing your e-mail account and skip to the "Sign Up with Facebook" section later in this chapter.

2 Type your password.

3 Click **Log In**.

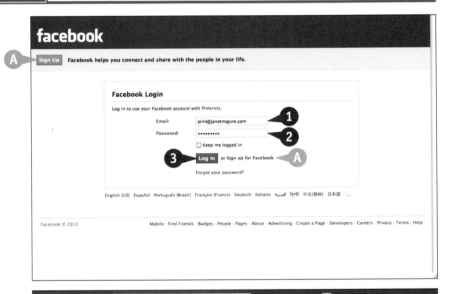

The Pinterest app window appears.

4 Click **Go to App**.

The Pinterest sign-up window appears.

5 Type a username for Pinterest.

6 Type your e-mail address.

7 Type a password.

8 Click **Create Account**.

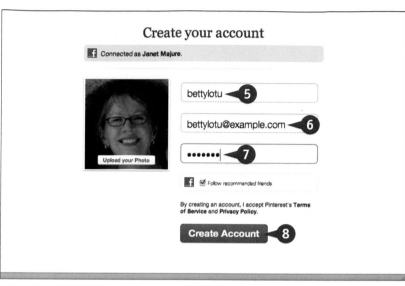

The Pinterest welcome screen opens.

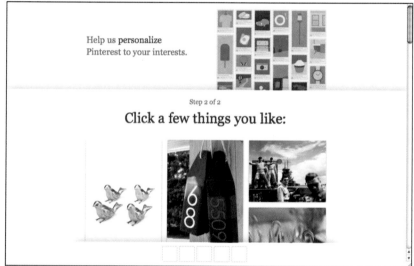

What is the advantage of using Facebook versus Twitter?

If you are active on Facebook, you may like the idea that your Pinterest selections can show up on Facebook and that your Facebook friends who use Pinterest automatically are available for you to follow on Pinterest. You can post links on Twitter to your Pinterest pins, but your pin images do not appear in your Twitter feed.

Join Pinterest Using Twitter

Y ou can use your existing Twitter account as an easy way to join Pinterest. Doing so makes signing up simple. On the first Pinterest sign-up page, you select Twitter as the way you want to sign up. You then provide your Twitter login information and give the two services authority to communicate your information with each other. If you do not have a Twitter account, you can sign up for one so as to join Pinterest.

Join Pinterest Using Twitter

1 In your internet browser, go to **https://pinterest.com/join/signup**.

2 Click **Twitter**.

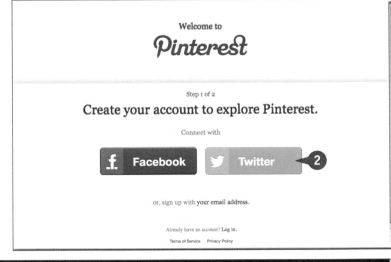

Twitter/Authorize an Application window opens.

3 Type your Twitter username or e-mail address in the Username box.

Ⓐ If you are not already a Twitter user, click **Sign up** instead of typing your information and skip to the "Sign Up with Twitter" section later in this chapter.

4 Type your Twitter password.

5 Click **Sign In**.

You are now signed into Twitter. The Create your account window appears.

6 Type a Pinterest username.

7 Type your e-mail address.

8 Type a password.

9 Click **Create Account**.

The Pinterest welcome screen opens. It will allow you to complete your sign-up.

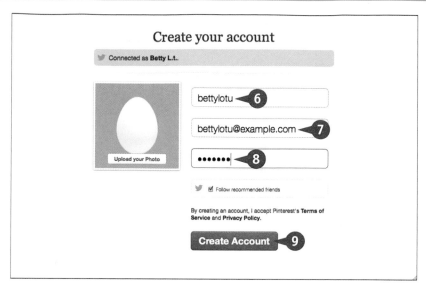

Is there any advantage to using Twitter instead of Facebook?
Twitter is the quicker and easier route. Twitter also is the way to go if you want to have a business Pinterest account or if you want to keep your Pinterest and personal Facebook accounts separate. Pinterest connects through personal Facebook accounts only, not through business pages.

Complete Your Sign-Up

After creating your Pinterest account using Facebook or Twitter, the welcome screen gives you a head start on a Pinterest *feed*, or presentation of new images, that is tailored to your interests. Pinterest leads you through the process. You click on five images that you like, click Continue, and then verify your e-mail address. After that, you are ready to start creating *boards* where you save images and collecting *pins*, or images that you want to save. If you do not complete this step immediately after creating your account, Pinterest directs you to the welcome page when you go to Pinterest.com.

Complete Your Sign-Up

1 On the welcome screen, click an image that you like.

2 Scroll down to see more images.

3 Click another image you like.

A Thumbnails of the images you select appear at the bottom of the screen.

4 Repeat Steps **2** and **3** until you have selected five images.

A red Continue button appears.

5 Click **Continue**.

B The Pinterest home page opens, with a note asking you to verify your email address.

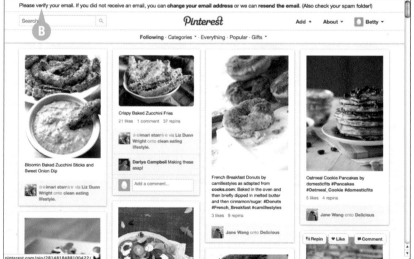

continued ▶

TIP

Should I click images based on whether I like the subject matter or on the quality of the image?
It probably is a good idea to lean toward selections whose subject matter appeals to you. Pinterest uses your choices to connect you with pinners whose collections Pinterest thinks you will like. When you finish your sign-up, you will be *following* those pinners, which means their new image selections appear in the feed you see by default when you are signed in at Pinterest.

When you complete your sign-up by verifying your e-mail address, you have access to all Pinterest member activities. Verifying your e-mail address requires you go to your e-mail inbox in the way you usually access your e-mail, opening the verification message from Pinterest, and then clicking a link in the message. Doing so confirms to Pinterest that the e-mail address you provided belongs to someone who wants to join Pinterest. Then, you can look at pinners that Pinterest thinks you would like.

Complete Your Sign-Up (continued)

⑥ Go to your e-mail account.

⑦ Open the e-mail message from Pinterest asking you to verify your email.

⑧ Click **Verify Email**.

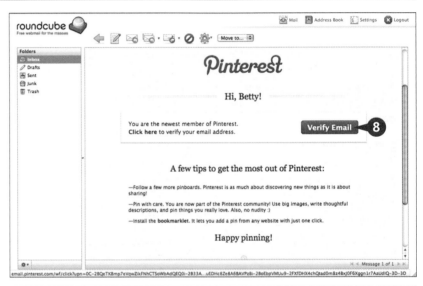

Your browser opens to the Pinterest home page with you logged in.

⑨ Click your name.

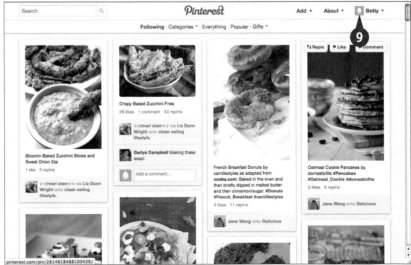

Your Pinterest profile page opens.

10 Click **Following**.

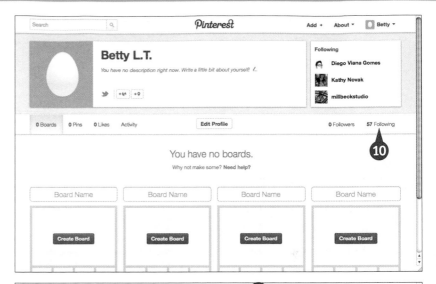

The profile page displays the following view.

11 Click **Unfollow** next to pinners whose pins you do not want to see in your personal default feed.

Ⓐ The Unfollow button changes to Follow.

12 Click **Pinterest**.

The Pinterest home page reappears and displays images from the pinners you are following.

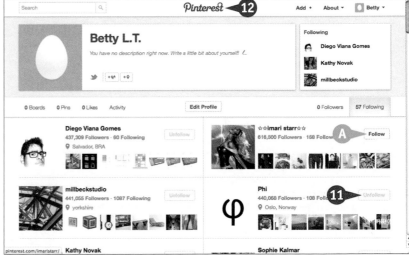

Why does Pinterest have me follow so many pinners?
Pinterest links you to a large number of popular pinners to give you a taste of the image possibilities in topics of interest to you. You are likely to be following pinners with hundreds of thousands of followers. You can continue to follow all of them or whittle them down to a few. If you prefer to see what the entire Pinterest community is pinning, you can click **Everything** under the Pinterest heading on the Pinterest home page.

Sign Up with Twitter

You can sign up with Pinterest by using your Twitter account, which is recommended for business pinners. Getting a Twitter account is simple and takes just a few moments. Of course, you can tweet if you want, too. With a link from Pinterest to Twitter, you can tell the Twitter world about images you have pinned. If you arrived at Twitter via a link from Pinterest, you may not be asked to follow all these steps, but they are recommended if you intend to tweet by sending messages through Twitter.

Sign Up with Twitter

1 In your Internet browser, go to **http://twitter.com**.

2 Type your name in the Full Name box.

3 Type your e-mail address.

4 Type a password.

5 Click **Sign up for Twitter**.

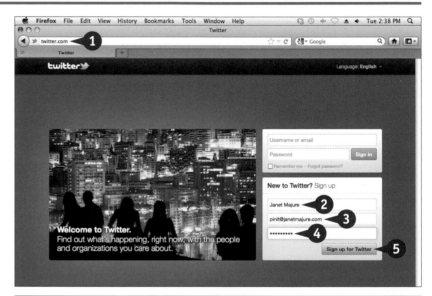

A confirmation screen appears.

6 Review the options and make any changes you desire.

7 When you are satisfied, click **Create my account**.

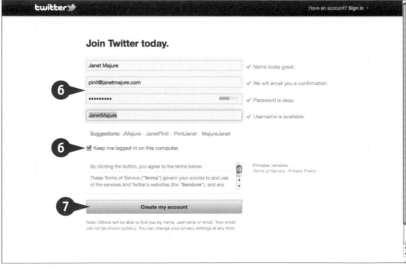

16

Twitter sends a confirmation e-mail to you and opens the welcome screen.

8 After reading the Twitter Teacher message, click **Next**.

Note: After signing up for a Twitter account, you are not required to post tweets to preserve the account. You can simply read those you follow or do nothing at all.

The Build Your Timeline window opens.

9 Click the **Follow** button next to anyone you want to follow.

A The Follow button changes to Following.

10 To find more possibilities, type a term in the Search box.

11 Click **Search**.

New options appear.

12 Repeat Step **9**.

13 Click **Next**.

Twitter shows a series of optional screens. Twitter sends you an e-mail message with a link to confirm your Twitter account.

TIP

Is there a way to try Twitter without broadcasting everything I post?
Yes, you can make your account private. While signed in, click your avatar image at the top of a Twitter page. Click **Settings** from the drop-down list. On the Account Settings page, click the **Protect my Tweets** check box (☐ changes to ☑), and your tweets will appear only to people you approve.

Sign Up with Facebook

You can register with Pinterest by using your Facebook account. If you do not have a Facebook account already, it is not a problem. Facebook is easy to join. You just need to have a valid e-mail address and provide some additional information. After completing the information on the Facebook sign-up screens, you receive a confirmation e-mail. It includes a link you need to click to finish the process. After that, you can use your Facebook logon information to sign into your Pinterest account.

Sign Up with Facebook

1 In your Internet browser, go to **www.facebook.com**.

2 Type your first name.

3 Type your last name.

4 Type your e-mail address.

5 Retype your e-mail address.

6 Type a password.

7 Click the down arrows (▾) and select your sex and birthday from the drop-down lists.

8 Click **Sign Up**.

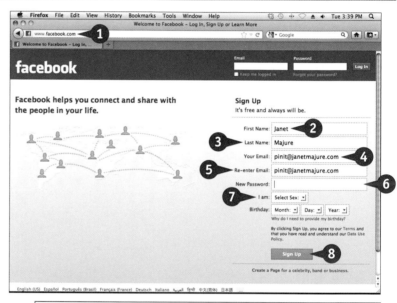

Your Facebook account is created, and you are taken to the Find your friends window.

9 Click **Skip this step** and then confirm your choice in the message box that appears.

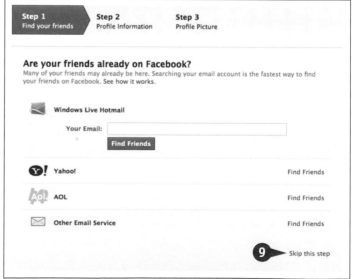

The Profile Information window opens.

⑩ Click **Skip**.

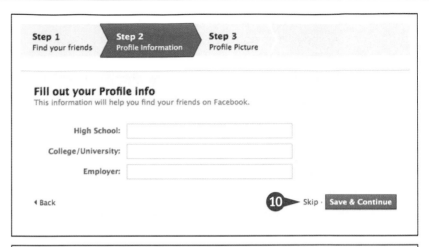

The Profile Picture window opens.

⑪ Click **Skip**.

Your profile page opens with a message to check your e-mail to complete the sign-up process.

TIPS

How do I validate my e-mail address with Facebook to complete my sign-up process?

To complete your sign-up process, check your e-mail account for an e-mail from Facebook. Open the e-mail and click the link to validate your e-mail address. Your account sign-up is now complete. Click **Okay**. Facebook reappears in your browser.

What should I do if I cannot find the confirmation e-mail sent by Facebook?

If you cannot find the e-mail sent by Facebook, check your Junk mailbox to see if it has been marked as spam. If the e-mail is not there, click the **Resend Email** button at the top of the Facebook interface.

Understanding Pinterest Terminology

You will be talking the Pinterest talk in no time once you learn a few terms and what they mean to Pinterest users. To understand Pinterest terminology, it is helpful to remember that the website is modeled on the idea of a bulletin board, or pinboard, on which people pin up images that they find useful, beautiful, or simply interesting. A few other terms are borrowed from other social media. They may sound odd at first, but they become second nature after just a little practice.

Pins, Pinning, and Pinners

A *pin* is an image that you select from your computer or a website, and *pinning* is the act of assigning a pin to your account. Thus, when you see a photo or other image that you adore, you pin it to a storage location, or pinboard, associated with your account. Posting a page torn from a magazine onto the bulletin board in your office is the physical world equivalent of pinning, and the magazine page is the equivalent of a pin on Pinterest. A *pinner* is the person who posts a pin.

Pinboards or Boards

Pinboards, or simply *boards*, are visual storage and organization spots where you keep your pins. You can name them, rearrange them, choose the cover pin for your board, and even have guests pin to your board. The boards constitute your personal pin categories. They are the Pinterest equivalent of the bulletin board at home where you pin up pictures of exercises that you want to remember to do or recipes that you want to try. Pinterest lets you have multiple boards, so you could have one for exercises and one for recipes.

Repin and Repinning

A *repin* is a pin to your board from someone else's board, and *repinning* is the act of adding a repin. Of course, people may repin images from your boards too. You could think of a repin as the photocopy you make of the craft idea a friend has placed on her refrigerator. Unlike photocopies, though, repins look as good as the original, and they carry their source information when you repin them.

Stool by Another Country.

dezeen.com

Follow and Followers

You can follow and be followed on Pinterest, meaning you can have another person's pins or another board's pins show up automatically when you are signed into

1 followers   **10 following**

Pinterest. By the same token, other pinners can follow you or a board that you keep.

Likes

Likes are little endorsements of pins that you enjoy but do not want to include on your pinboards. When you click Like on a pin, Pinterest remembers that you liked it, so you can access it through your account even though it is not on a board. Using *like* as a noun feels awkward at first, but most people become used to it quickly, even if they do not like using the word that way.

Easy and beautifull...

10 likes   52 repins

Andreia Catela onto Wedding Ideas

Log into Pinterest Three Ways

Once you have an account, logging into Pinterest gives you access to pinning, commenting, and more. Logging in is easy, but the login screen can be confusing at first. That is because the Pinterest login screen gives you three different ways to log in. You always can use your e-mail address for logging in. Depending on whether you connected to Pinterest through Facebook or Twitter, you also can use one or both of them to sign in. Whichever way you log in, you have full access to your account. Choose any of the following methods for logging in.

Log into Pinterest Three Ways

Login with Pinterest E-mail

1 In your browser, go to **http://pinterest.com**.

2 Click **Login**.

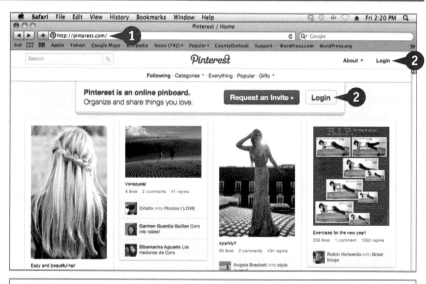

The Pinterest login screen appears.

3 Type the e-mail address that you used when you signed up for Pinterest in the e-mail box.

4 Type your Pinterest password.

5 Click **Login**.

Your personal Pinterest home page opens.

Login with Facebook

1 Repeat Steps **1** and **2**.

2 Click **Login with Facebook**.

3 In the Facebook Login screen, type in your Facebook e-mail address.

4 Type your Facebook password.

5 Click **Log In**.

Your personal Pinterest home page opens.

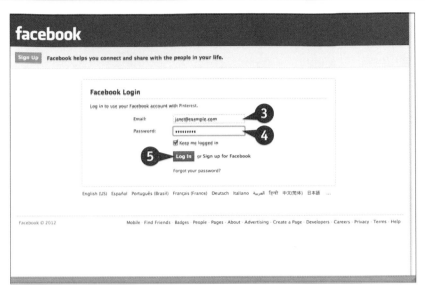

Login with Twitter

1 Repeat Steps **1** and **2**.

2 Click **Login with Twitter**.

3 In the Twitter login screen, type your Twitter e-mail address or username.

4 Type your Twitter password.

5 Click **Sign In**.

Your personal Pinterest home page opens.

TIPS

Why did Pinterest log me in automatically when I clicked Login with Facebook?

If you are already logged into your Facebook account in the browser where you went to Pinterest, simply clicking the **Login with Facebook** button at Pinterest picks up your Facebook login from your browser. The same is true for Twitter.

Do my Pinterest e-mail and password need to be the same as the credentials that I use with Facebook or Twitter?

No, your e-mail and password can be different for each site. Using the same e-mail address is usually not a problem. However, many security consultants say using the same password across multiple websites endangers your online security.

23

Create a Bio

You can let your fellow Pinterest members know a little more about you when you post a mini biography of yourself. Your biography can mention your interests and other details that may help Pinterest members determine whether you are a pinner who they would like to follow. You also can show your location and link to your website, if you have one. Because your Pinterest bio is entirely public, it is best to focus on information you are willing to let the world know and avoid including personal information that could compromise your security.

Create a Bio

1 In your browser, go to **http://pinterest.com**.

2 Click your name in the title bar.

3 Click the area under your name, and type a brief bio.

4 Click **Save Description**.

Pinterest saves the bio.

5 Click the **Globe** button (🌐) if you have a personal website or blog.

A box with a check mark appears.

6 Type your personal website or blog address in the box.

7 Click the check mark option (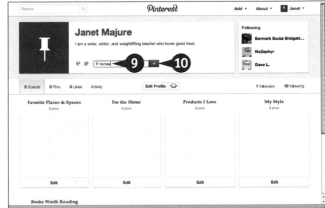) to confirm the address.

The box closes. Pinterest saves the URL, and others will able to click the icon to go to your website.

8 Click the **Map pin** button (+9).

A box with a check mark option appears.

9 Type the name of your location in the blank.

10 Click the check mark () to confirm your location.

The box closes, and the map pin icon appears beside the other icons.

TIP

Is there any other way to record this information?

Yes. You can click the **Edit Profile** button on your profile page, or click your name and select **Settings** from the drop-down list. These both take you to the Edit Profile page, which provides an About box, where you can enter your bio or description, a Location box for the location, a Website box, and more.

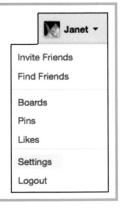

Upload a Profile Picture

You can upload a picture from your computer to give the Pinterest community a sense of your personality or interests. If you have a profile picture with the Facebook or Twitter account that you used to sign up with Pinterest, then Pinterest uses that image by default. However, you may prefer to have a different picture associated with your Pinterest profile. When selecting an image to upload, keep in mind that it will display as a square. You can crop it on your computer to that shape, or Pinterest crops it for you automatically.

Upload a Profile Picture

1 On the Pinterest home page, click your name.

2 On your profile page, click **Edit Profile**.

The Edit Profile page opens.

3 Scroll down until you see the red pushpin image.

4 Click **Upload an Image**.

The button changes to a box with a Browse button.

5 Click **Browse**.

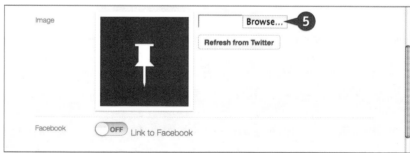

Your browser opens a window for locating the image of your choice.

6 Click the image you want.

7 Click **Open.**

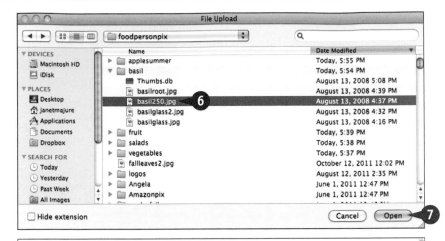

Ⓐ Pinterest uploads the image in the Image box.

8 Scroll to the bottom of the page.

9 Click **Save Profile**.

Your new profile image is saved and active.

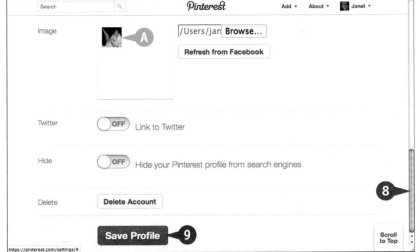

Is there something I should do to my picture, because it shows up as a very small image in the Image box?

Your picture probably is fine. After you save, Pinterest returns you to your profile page. The image should appear at the appropriate size next to your bio there. If it does not, choose a larger image.

How can I adjust the way Pinterest crops my profile image?

You cannot alter the way Pinterest crops your picture, but you can crop it on your own computer before you upload it. In Windows, you can use the free Paint program that is in the Accessories portion of your Programs directory. On a Mac, you can use the Preview program.

Install a Bookmarklet

The easiest way to pin to your board, apart from repinning, is to use the Pinterest bookmarklet. The *bookmarklet* is a tiny script that enables your browser to identify an image on a web page that you can pin to your Pinterest boards. Installing the bookmarklet is easy, too. For some browsers, all you need to do is drag the bookmarklet from Pinterest onto your toolbar. It takes only a moment and saves you a lot of effort when you want to create a new pin.

Install a Bookmarklet

Install in Firefox

1 Click **View.**

2 Click **Toolbars.**

3 Click **Bookmarks Toolbar.**

The Bookmarks toolbar appears under the address box.

4 Type **http://pinterest.com/about/goodies** in your browser.

Note: You can get there by clicking **Pin It** button under the About menu on the Pinterest home page.

5 Click and drag the **Pin It** button from the web page onto the Firefox bookmarks toolbar.

Note: Release the mouse button when the Pin It button reaches the Firefox bookmarks toolbar.

The Pin It bookmarklet is installed and ready to use.

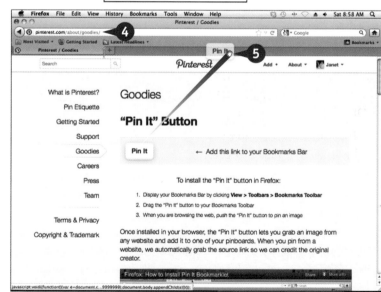

Install in Chrome

1 Click **View**.

2 Click **Always Show Bookmarks Bar**.

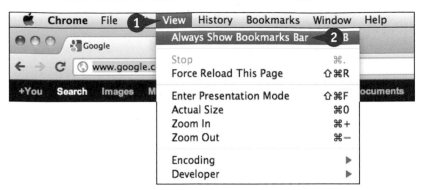

The bookmarks bar expands.

3 Type **http://pinterest.com/about/goodies** in your browser.

Note: You can get there by clicking **Pin It** button under the About menu on the Pinterest home page.

4 Click and drag the **Pin It** button from the web page onto the Chrome bookmarks toolbar.

Note: Release the mouse button when the Pin It button reaches the Chrome bookmarks toolbar.

The Pin It bookmarklet is installed and ready to use.

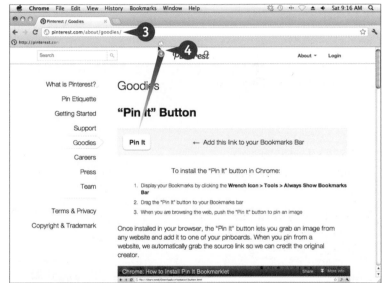

How do I install the bookmarklet with Internet Explorer?

Type **http://pinterest.com/about/goodies** in the Explorer address bar. Press Enter. Below the address bar, a tab shows the name of the current web page. Tabs for other pages may be present. Right-click in the area next to the tabs. Click **Favorites bar** if it does not have a check mark next to it. The Favorites bar appears. Right-click the **Pin It** bookmarklet. Select **Add to Favorites**. A message box opens. Click the **Create In** arrow. Select **Favorites Bar** from the drop-down list. Click **Add**. The bookmarklet appears on the Favorites bar.

Understanding Pinterest Etiquette

When you follow the rules of etiquette as defined by Pinterest, you are sure to get along with the Pinterest community and have fun while you do it. Pinterest includes three simple rules of etiquette when it sends you a welcome e-mail message, and it lists two more on its etiquette page, http://pinterest.com/about/etiquette/. You probably will appreciate the etiquette and enforcement of the rules if you prefer a place that has a positive tone and a minimum of adult material.

Official Etiquette

When you joined Pinterest, you probably got an e-mail listing three rules of Pinterest etiquette: be respectful, be authentic, and credit your sources. The Pin Etiquette page, at http://pinterest.com/about/etiquette, adds these: report objectionable content and tell how to make Pinterest better. The additional two rules of etiquette are important to help Pinterest enforce the rules overall. You and other members of the Pinterest community, as well as sources of pins, gain more benefit from the site when you follow the rules.

What is Pinterest?

Pin Etiquette

Acceptable Use Policy

In case you did not read the Terms of Service when you signed up with Pinterest, be advised that when you opened your account, you agreed to follow the official etiquette as well as the Acceptable Use Policy at http://pinterest.com/about/use/. The policy stipulates, among other things, that you will not post content that could harm any person, animal, or property, or exploit children. It also forbids spam as well as violent and hateful content. You probably have no intention of posting any such material, but if you do pin something questionable, it might disappear, at least temporarily.

Acceptable Use Policy

In Practical Terms

Besides the explicit ban on nudity, in practical terms the etiquette and use policy means Pinterest bans pro-anorexia pins, as an example of pins deemed harmful to people. Pinterest reviews and removes offending pins. It also blocks links from pins that go to Amazon and other online businesses that pay

Sorry!
Users have reported that this links to spam or other inappropriate content.
Back to Pinterest

commissions through what are known as associate programs. You can help keep Pinterest friendly by reporting questionable pins. Pinterest includes a button on each pin's page that you can click to report it.

Etiquette Pros & Cons

In the freewheeling world of the Internet, some people may chafe at the etiquette required on Pinterest. Those people argue that the rules interfere with freedom of speech and turn members into squealers. Etiquette supporters believe that the rules support people who produce the images that appear on Pinterest.

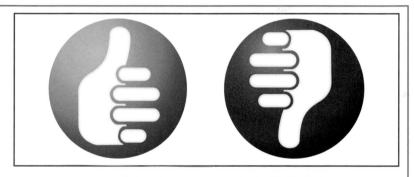

They also say that the rules reduce hatefulness and negativity — major turnoffs for most people —and thus make Pinterest a bit of a refuge compared with many interactive websites.

Unofficial Etiquette

In addition to the official Pinterest rules of etiquette are some unofficial rules to keep in mind. The main unofficial rule, especially if you like having followers, is to pin high-quality pictures. In other words, aim for images that are in focus and well lit. Although it is not forbidden, Pinterest is not intended as the place

You haven't liked any pins yet.

to pin fuzzy pictures of your child's kindergarten play. Another good rule is to engage others by writing thank-you comments where appropriate, using the Like button, and inviting friends. Pinterest is evolving and more unofficial rules are likely to develop.

Create a New Board

You need at least one board to start pinning. If you did not create any boards when you signed up, you can do so now. If you did create some, you can add new boards to expand your collections and organize them. Pinterest offers several ways to add boards. You can create a board from the Add+ link at the top of nearly all Pinterest pages. You also can add boards on the fly. That is, you may decide as you are creating a pin that you want to place it on a new board. Pinterest lets you do just that.

Create a New Board

1 At the top of a Pinterest page, click **your name.**

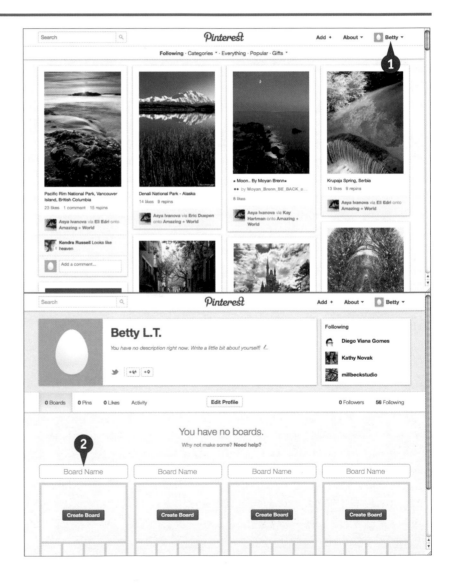

Your profile page opens.

2 Click a **Board Name** box.

The box goes blank and a cursor appears.

3 Type a name for your board.

4 Click **Create Board**.

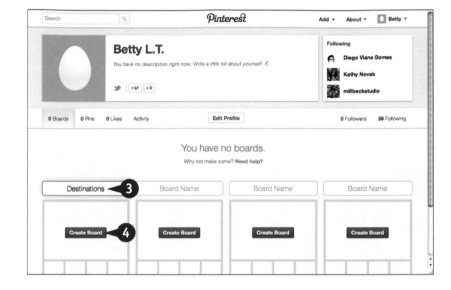

A A blank board page appears.

5 Repeat Steps **2** to **4** creating up to three more boards.

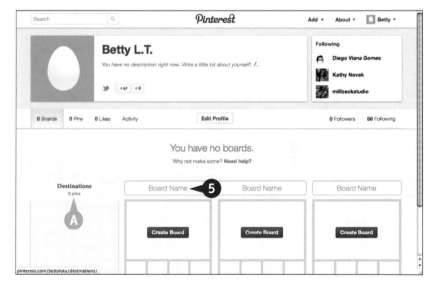

How many boards should I create?
You need enough boards to organize your pin collections, but not so many that you lose track. It is probably better to start with a few and then add boards when you find yourself wanting to segregate some pins.

What do I do if none of the categories seems to fit the board I am creating?
You have two options. You can skip choosing a category and then assign it a category later. Or you can choose a category that you are not sure about, or even choose the catchall Other category, and change it later if you want.

Create Your First Pin

When you create your first pin, you are on your way to collecting the images you want to organize in categories, use to plan activities, or simply enjoy. You can create your first pin from a site on the Internet by doing little more than copying and pasting the URL where the image appears. Pinning from a URL can be especially handy if you have a list of URLs of favorite images, such as one created using your browser's Favorites or Bookmarks feature. You need a URL for a specific web page, not just a domain, such as *example.com*, for best results.

Create Your First Pin

1 On the Pinterest home page, click **Add+**.

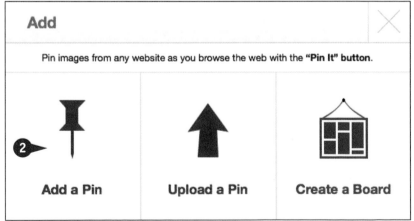

The Add window opens.

2 Click **Add a Pin**.

The Add a Pin window opens.

3 Type the desired URL in the box.

4 Click **Find Images**.

The Add a Pin window changes.

A If you change your mind, you can close the window by clicking the **X**.

B The image box displays images from the URL one at a time.

5 Click **Next** until you find the image you want.

6 Click the **Board** down arrow (▾) and select the board where you want the image to appear from the drop-down list.

7 Type a description in the box.

8 Click **Pin It**.

The window tells you it is pinning and then opens the pin's page at Pinterest.

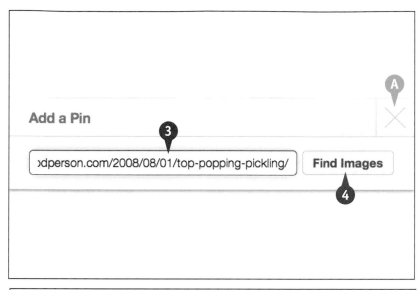

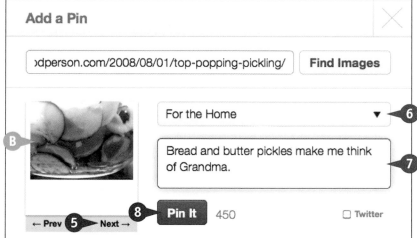

TIPS

Can I type a domain's URL and click through all images on the domain?
No. When you enter the domain only, the Add a Pin window shows only the images on the domain's home page.

Why can I not see any images when I entered a URL for a web page where I know there are images?
The site may be blocking Pinterest pins or the images may be in frames. Try entering the exact URL of the image itself, such as by right-clicking the image and choosing **Copy Image Location**.

Create a Pin from the Pin It Bookmarklet

The quickest and easiest way to create a pin is by using the Pin It bookmarklet. Once you have installed the bookmarklet, you can pin while viewing your favorite websites. When you see an image you like, you click the bookmarklet. It then lets you select the image, choose a board where you want to keep it, create a description for the image, and then pin it — all without leaving the site where the image appears. If you do not have the bookmarklet, see the "Install a Bookmarklet" section in this chapter.

Create a Pin from the Pin It Bookmarklet

1 When you see a picture you like on a web page, click the **Pin It** bookmarklet.

The screen changes and presents all the images on the web page available for pinning.

2 Position your mouse ▸ over the image you want.

The Pin This button appears over the image.

3 Click **Pin This**.

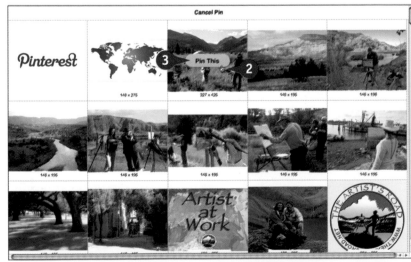

The Create Pin window
opens.

④ Click the **Board** down
arrow (▾) and select a
board from the drop-down
list.

⑤ Type a brief description.

⑥ Click **Pin It**.

The Create Pin window
confirms the pin.

⑦ Click **See your Pin**.

The bookmarklet opens a
new tab in your browser,
showing your new pin on
your Pinterest board.

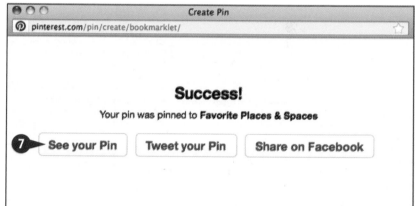

Is there an easier way to get a description for the image?

If you select text on the web page before you click the bookmarklet, the text appears in the description box when you click **Pin It** in the image selection view. Also, an image may have text associated with it that you ordinarily do not see in your browser. In such a case, the associated text automatically appears in the description box.

Why does the image I want to pin not show up with the bookmarklet?

An image may not appear because it is smaller than the minimum of 80-by-80 pixels or the owner has blocked the image from pinning. You need to find a different image. An image embedded in an iframe, which is common on Tumblr, also may not appear with the bookmarklet. You may be able to pin it by copying the image's URL and pasting it using the Add+ button at Pinterest. Right-click the image, and select **Copy Image Location** to copy the URL.

CHAPTER 2

Navigating Pinterest

Now that you are up and running with Pinterest, it is time to find your way around. Pinterest gives you lots of ways to navigate the site to find things you like, people whose interests you share, and more.

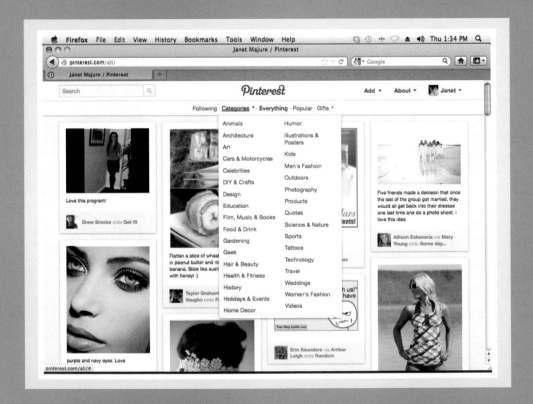

Find Pins with Everything and Popular

Y ou can easily find images that you want to keep, or *pin,* by viewing the images, also known as *pins*, on Pinterest. Pinterest makes it easy when you go to the home page at http://pinterest. com. It shows a cascade, or *feed*, of images that other people have pinned. You can view all the latest pins. If you prefer, you can view pins in specific categories that interest you or view only the most popular recent pins. Popularity is based on the number of times people have repinned the image or clicked its Like button.

Find Pins with Everything and Popular

1 In your browser, type **http:// pinterest.com** and press **Enter** (**Return**).

Note: By default, Pinterest shows pins from people you are following on the home page when you are logged in.

2 Click **Everything**.

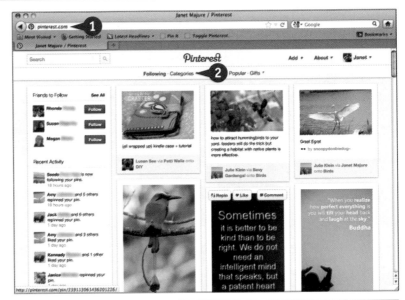

The page displays the latest pins.

Ⓐ The URL reads pinterest.com/ all/, so you know you are seeing the latest pins.

3 Position your mouse ⬏ over Categories.

4 Click a category that interests you.

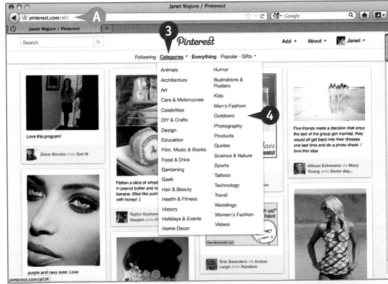

The stream of images changes to those marked in the category of your choice.

Note: This example is the Outdoors category.

5 Scroll down to see all the latest pins in that category.

B The URL confirms the category you are viewing.

C The Scroll to Top tab sends you to the top of the page if you click it.

6 Click **Popular**.

The latest popular images appear on the screen, allowing you to scroll through them.

D The URL confirms you are on the Popular feed.

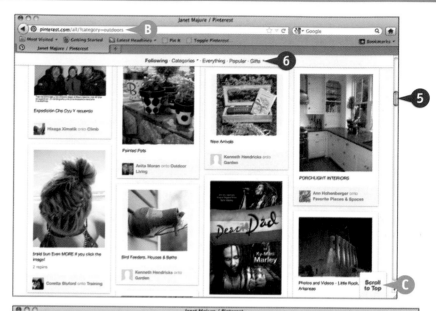

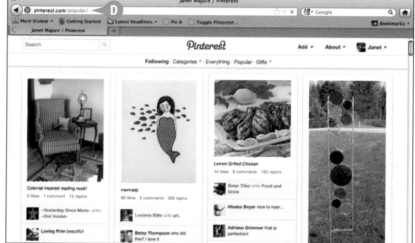

When I pin things, do they automatically show up in the Everything feed?

Not necessarily. In an effort to combat spam pins, Pinterest has indicated that it may hold off on displaying the pins of new users until it is apparent the new users are legitimate.

Can I look at pins this way without logging in?

You can view the Everything pins, the Popular pins, and pins by category when you are not logged in. The Everything view, or *feed*, is the default view in that case. If you are not logged in, you cannot view a feed based on pinners you follow.

Find Pins with Pinterest Search

APinterest search allows you to do a more precise search for what you want, whereas the Everything and Popular feeds may be better for discovery, or finding things you did not even know you were seeking. A Pinterest search box appears at the top of most Pinterest pages. You can type a word or words in the search box, and Pinterest presents a feed based on your search terms plus links to pinners and boards based on those terms.

Find Pins with Pinterest Search

① Click in the search box, and type your search term.

② Click the **Search** button (🔍), or press Enter (Return).

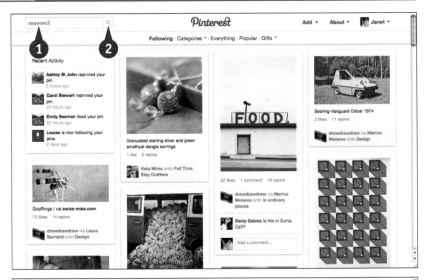

Pinterest displays pins that include the search term and provides additional links.

③ Click **Boards**.

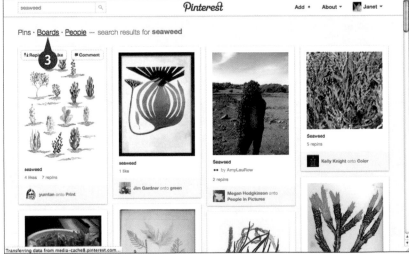

A display of boards that use the search term appears.

Ⓐ Clicking the name on a board takes you to the page where you can see that board in its entirety.

④ Click **People**.

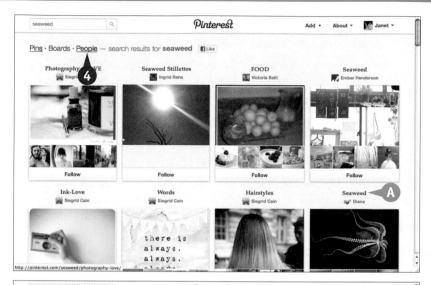

Pinterest displays people whose names or usernames include the search term.

⑤ Click the person's image to go to her page.

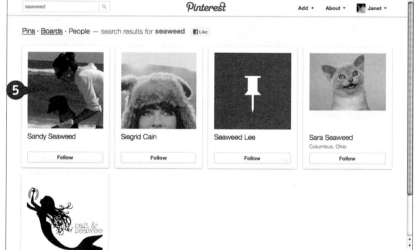

Are there other ways to search for images that I may want to pin?
You can try a Google search of the Pinterest site, which may provide slightly different results. To do so, type your search term in a Google search box followed by **site:pinterest.com**. For example, you could type *seaweed* **site:pinterest.com**. When Google brings up results, click **Images** in the left sidebar of your browser window, and you will see images relating to the search term from Pinterest.

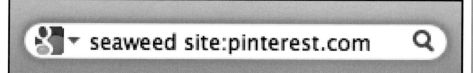

Follow a Pinner

You create your own customized feed when you follow pinners. That is, when you are signed into Pinterest and go to the Pinterest home page, the default feed you see is Pinners You Follow. Because all Pinterest activity involves boards, following a pinner really means following all boards that the pinner maintains. To the extent that you follow pinners who share your interests or tastes, you see pins that align with those interests. You also may choose to follow a pinner whose style differs markedly from yours, all the better to broaden your perspective.

Follow a Pinner

1 After you identify a pinner who interests you, click the pinner's name under a recent pin.

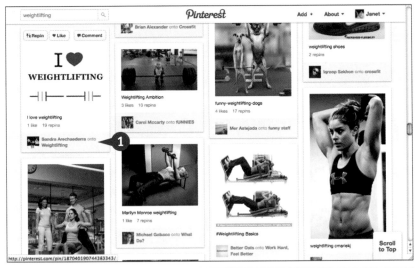

The pinner's page opens.

2 Scroll through the pinner's list of boards to see if you really want to follow the pinner.

Note: You can choose to follow boards instead of pinners, as explained in the section, "Follow a Board."

3 If you want to follow the pinner, click **Follow All**.

Ⓐ The Follow All button changes to read Unfollow All.

④ Click your name.

Your profile page opens.

⑤ Click **Following**.

The page changes to reveal all the pinners you are following.

⑥ Scroll through the list of who you are following to confirm that the pinner you newly added appears there.

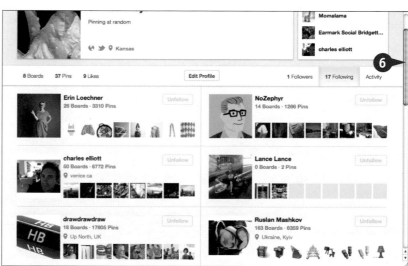

Do I need to obtain permission from an individual to follow the person?
No. Unlike Facebook, you can get the feed of anyone who pins. When you decide to follow a pinner, that person receives a notification by e-mail from Pinterest of your decision and also in the activity box that appears on the Pinterest home page. Of course, that means anyone can view your pins, too, which is a good idea to keep in mind as you pin.

Follow a Board

Just as you can follow a pinner, you also can follow a specific board. When you follow a board rather than follow a pinner, meaning all boards from that pinner, you can fine-tune the content of your personal default feed on the Pinterest home page. Perhaps you have a friend who pins cool ideas for making sculptures from castoff items, but also pins images of stuffed animals, which you abhor. Rather than following that friend's entire feed, you can follow only his Repurposeful Sculptures feed. The first step is to find a board you want to follow.

Follow a Board

1 After you identify a board that you want to follow, click the board name under a pinned image for that board.

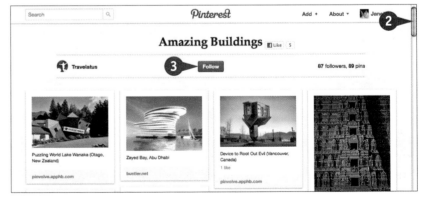

The board's page opens.

2 Scroll through the pins to confirm the board you want to follow.

3 If you are sure that you want to follow the board, click **Follow** near the top of the page.

Ⓐ The Follow button changes to Unfollow.

④ Click your name.

Your profile page opens.

⑤ Click **Following.**

The page changes to reveal all the pinners you are following.

⑥ Scroll down to find the pinner for the new board you are following.

Note: The pinner, and not the board, is listed.

Ⓑ You can tell you are following a board or boards, not the pinner, because the Follow button is available should you want to follow all boards by that person.

What is the best way to determine which boards to follow?
One good way is not to follow boards at first. Instead, view pins from the general community and repin the ones you love. If you see the same board from the same pinner appearing a lot among your repins, it is probably is a good choice for you to follow.

Find Pinners via Related Sites

Visiting some sites that talk *about* Pinterest is a great way to discover other Pinterest users, or *pinners*, whom you might like to follow. Some sites show the most popular pinners, but others show pinners who are especially valuable if you share their particular interests. The sites listed here are great places to start, but more are sure to pop up as Pinterest becomes more established. Some sites have Pinterest as a subject. One good one is http://mashable.com/follow/topics/pinterest.

The Big Picture

The website Zoomsphere.com maintains a list of the most popular pinners across Pinterest at www.zoomsphere.com/charts/pinterest/all. It updates daily and shows the most popular pinners based on the total number of followers as well as which pinners are gaining followers fastest. The site provides multiple ways to look at the data with a set of drop-down lists. The lists let you specify that you want to see popularity based on pins or on *likes*; that is, the pinners whose pins have garnered the most clicks on the Like button. You also can choose to view data by country and by change in popularity across different time frames.

The Even Bigger Picture

On its home page at www.repinly.com, the website Repinly shows the most popular pinners by number of followers, the most-followed boards by category, pins that are being repinned by many users, and more. The site presents statistics in a quick, visual fashion appropriate for Pinterest lovers. At the bottom of the Repinly home page is the link More Popular Boards. Try clicking it, or go straight to www.repinly.com/popular_boards. aspx to find a long list of popular boards. Unless you have especially unusual interests, you are sure to find pinners or boards to follow on this site.

Get a Look at Fashions

Fashion is a hot topic on Pinterest, so it is not surprising that the fashion site www.stylelist.com keeps its readers up to date on style-worthy pinners to follow. The site updates its list about once a week, and manages to find new pinners to highlight. Along with brief descriptions of why you might want to follow the selected pinners are links to their profiles on Pinterest. Find the latest at www.stylelist.com/tag/stylelist-hot-on-pinterest.

STYLELIST HOT ON PINTEREST

Teachers Share Tips

If you are a teacher, you can get a list of educators to follow at Education World. The list, at www.educationworld.com/a_curr/pinterest-power-pinners.html, lists five pinners whose pins offer a wealth of ideas, from special events to Dr. Seuss. You can go to Education World's own page on Pinterest, at http://pinterest.com/educationworld. From there, you can follow Education World or a few of its boards. You get more ideas when you click Following and see what pinners Education World is following.

EducationWorld®
The Educator's Best Friend™

Mashable Offerings

For an eclectic list of pinners, as selected by editors at Mashable, go to mashable.com/2012/01/29/pinterest-users-to-follow and view "21 Must-Follow Users." The list includes pinners specializing in photography, gifts, architecture, weddings, travel, and more. It is a fun list, and Mashable presents its selections in a series of slides. Each slide features an image from one pinner and names the Mashable editors' favorite board from that pinner. The pinner's name links to his Pinterest page.

The Pinners Board at Pinterest

Unsurprisingly, there is a pinboard at Pinterest dedicated to lists of pinners. That board, at pinterest.com/ladypinsalot/pinners, provides images that link to websites that offer lists of recommended pinners in a variety of subjects. They include lists of suggested pinners for designers and for e-book fans plus lists of food-loving pinners, techy pinners, and blogging crafters who pin. You can click the pins and make your way to the original image. Of course, you also can follow this particular board so that any time Lady Pinsalot posts a new list, it appears in your feed.

Repin a Pin

By far the most popular way to pin images to your boards is by repinning someone else's pins. *Repinning*, to be clear, is adding a pin to your board from elsewhere on Pinterest, whereas *pinning* is putting an image from another site or your computer onto Pinterest. Repinning is the simplest way to add to your boards, as Pinterest offers immediate access to a wide array of remarkable images. You can even repin from your own collection of pins. For example, you could repin a knitted baby sweater that you have on your Knitting board to your Baby Things board.

Repin a Pin

1 Position your mouse ▶ over an image of interest, which makes the Repin, Like, and Comment buttons appear.

2 Click **Repin**.

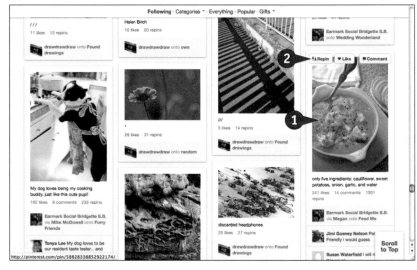

The Repin window opens.

3 Click the **Repin** down arrow (▾) and select a board from the drop-down list.

4 Click in the box to edit the description that came from the original pin.

5 Click **Pin It**.

Pinterest adds the image to your board and briefly displays a message telling you before returning you to the main menu.

6 Scroll to the top of the main page.

7 Click your name.

8 Click **Pins** in the drop-down list.

Your Pins page appears, showing your selection.

A Your selection is labeled Repinned and displays the board you pinned it to and the original source of the pin.

9 To repin your repin to another of your boards, position your mouse ↖ over the image to display the Repin, Like, and Comment buttons.

10 Click **Repin**.

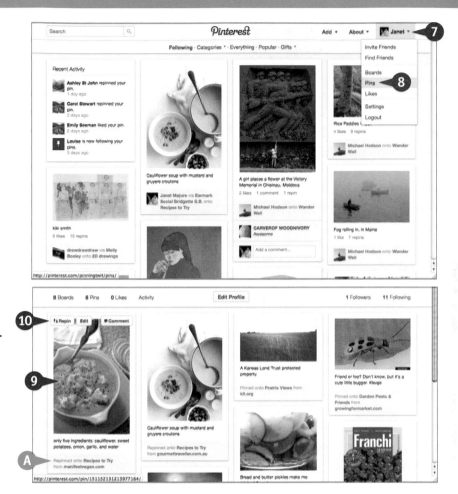

TIP

What is the purpose of the repin confirmation that appeared and then disappeared so fast?

The repin confirmation provides immediate access to the relevant board or pin. If you were quick, you saw that it read, "Repinned to [*the name of your board*]. Shared with your followers. See it now." Both the board's name and See it now are active links. You can click these links to go to the board or the pin if you respond quickly.

> **Repin** ✕
>
> Repinned to **Recipes to Try.**
>
> Shared with your followers. **See it now.**

Understanding the Pin Window

When you click an image, you can get a lot of information about the pin. That is true for images in feeds as well as on your profile and pins pages. Simply click the image itself, rather than clicking one of the buttons that appears when you hold your mouse pointer over it. The Pin window appears on top of the page you were viewing and gives you access to various ways to share an image, repin it, like it, and find related pins.

Top of the Window

Ⓐ The pinner's name

Ⓑ Time image was pinned

Ⓒ Source of image

Ⓓ Unfollow/Follow button, should you want to unfollow or follow the pinner

Ⓔ A large version of the image, with the pinner's description under it

Ⓕ Social sharing buttons

Ⓖ Button that displays code for placing image on your website

Ⓗ Button for reporting inappropriate pin

Ⓘ Button to e-mail image link

Bottom of Window

A Comments about the pin

B Link to report inappropriate comments

C A space to add your own comments

D The pin's board summary, including thumbnails of other pins and an Unfollow/Follow button

E The pinner's summary, including thumbnails and Unfollow/Follow button

F A summary of pin's source

A Sampling of repinners, with links to the people and the board where they repinned the image

B Link to more repinners

C Thumbnails of people who liked the pin, with links to their profiles and to more likes

Like a Pin

Y ou can like a pin, even if you do not want to add it to your boards. Maybe you want to show support for the pinner. Maybe you have not decided whether to pin it. *Liking*, or clicking the image's Like button, lets you do both. There are multiple ways to like a pin. After you have liked it, you can find the pin again by clicking the Likes link on your profile page. Then, you can simply view it or, if you prefer, you can pin it to a board or even *unlike* it. That is, you can undo your like.

Like a Pin

On a Pinterest Feed

1 Position your mouse ▶ over the desired image.

The Repin, Like, and Comment buttons appear.

2 Click **Like**.

The Like button changes to Unlike.

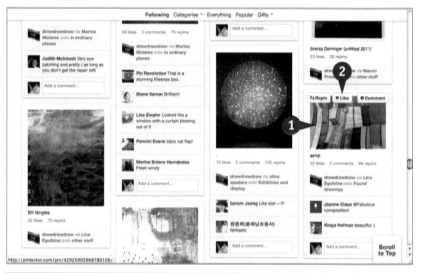

On a Pin's Page

1 Position your mouse ▶ over the image.

The Repin and Like buttons appear.

2 Click **Like**.

The Like button changes to Unlike.

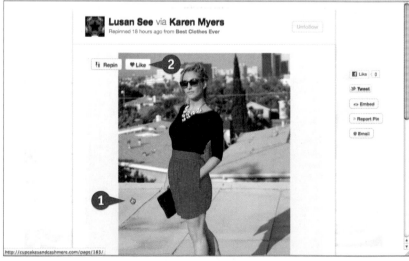

Liking on Facebook

1 On the pin's page, click the Facebook **Like** button.

The Facebook sign-in window opens.

2 Type your Facebook e-mail address.

3 Type your Facebook password.

4 Click **Log In**.

You are logged into Facebook and returned to the pin page.

5 Click the Facebook **Like** button.

The button dims and the number beside it increases by one.

Where do the pins go after I like them?

If you used the Pinterest Like function, the pins become part of your Pinterest record. To see your likes, click **Likes** on your profile page, accessible via your name at the top of the Pinterest page. Alternatively, click **Likes** under the drop-down list. The Facebook like shows up as a Facebook thumbs-up on your Facebook page. Your Pinterest likes also may show up on Facebook, as explained in Chapters 8 and 10.

Comment on a Pin

If liking and pinning are not enough for you, you can add your two cents with a comment. To do so, you click the Comment button and start writing. Remember to make your remarks respectful to keep in the Pinterest spirit. Comments appear with the pin or the repin where you leave them. Therefore, if you comment on someone's repin, those comments appear only with that repin and not with the original pin or with subsequent repins.

Comment on a Pin

In a Feed

1 Position your mouse ⬉ over an image and click the **Comment** button when it appears.

A comment box appears next to your profile picture.

2 Type your comment in the box.

3 Click **Comment**.

Your comment appears under the image, and a new comment box appears next to your profile picture.

Note: A comment box appears automatically if other comments exist.

On a Pin's Page

1 Type your comment in the box that appears automatically under the image and any displayed comments.

2 Click **Post Comment**.

Your comment appears under the image, and a new comment box appears.

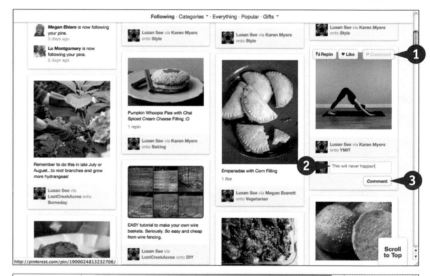

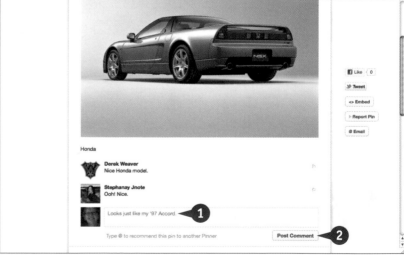

View Your Comments

1 Click your name at the top of any Pinterest page to go to your profile page.

2 On your profile page, click **Activity**.

Ⓐ Comments you have made appear over the pertinent images.

View All Comments

1 Scroll to the bottom of the displayed comments.

2 Click **All *N* comments** where *N* is the total number of comments.

Pinterest displays the pin's page and all the comments.

TIP

Why does my comment show up on my activity page, but not on the original pin?

If you repinned the image before you commented, then you may have commented on your repin, rather than on the original pin. Look at the pin on your board to see if your comment appears there. The absence of the comment also could be due to processing delays at Pinterest. In addition, to reduce spam Pinterest sometimes does not publish pins for new pinners until it is sure they are legitimate.

Unfollow a Pinner

You can unfollow a pinner if you decide you do not share that person's interests or tastes or if the feed from that pinner is overwhelming your feed page. You can unfollow from your profile page, or you can do it from the pinner's page, a good option if you want to review the boards before unfollowing. If you have several pinners you want to unfollow, however, you can do so only one at a time.

Unfollow a Pinner

From Your Profile Page

1 On your profile page, click **Following**.

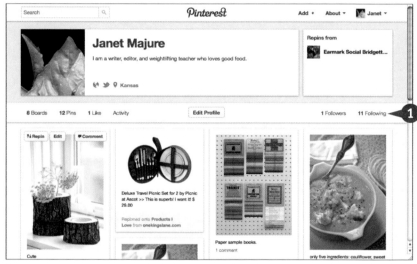

Pinterest displays all the pinners you are following.

2 Scroll down until you see the pinner who you want to unfollow.

3 Click **Unfollow**.

The Unfollow button changes to Follow.

Note: At this stage, you can click Follow to resume following the pinner.

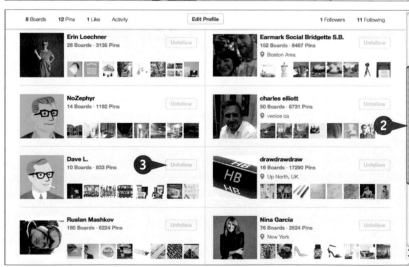

From the Pinner's Profile Page

1 Repeat Steps **1** and **2** in this section.

2 Click the pinner's name or profile image.

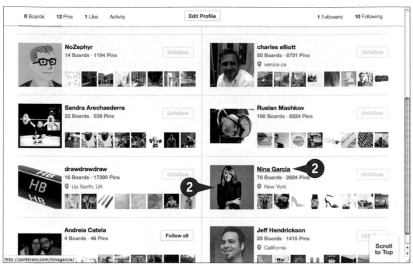

Pinterest displays the pinner's profile page.

3 Scroll down to review the boards.

4 Click **Pins** to review individual pins.

5 When you are satisfied that you want to unfollow the pinner, click **Unfollow All**.

The Unfollow All button changes to Follow All.

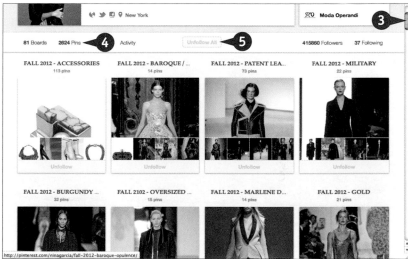

TIP

Is there a difference between the Unfollow button associated with pinners on my profile's Following page and the Unfollow All button that appears when I go to the pinner's profile page?

Those buttons give the same results. The different terminology reflects the fact that unfollowing differs based on location. On the pinner's profile page, individual Unfollow buttons appear under each board. By including *All*, the large Unfollow All top button clearly distinguishes itself from the individual Unfollow buttons. On your Following page, you cannot unfollow individual boards, only the pinner. Therefore, the Unfollow button does not need the added *All*.

59

Unfollow a Board

As you get more familiar with the boards you are following, you may want to make adjustments. The pinners and boards you follow, you may remember, form the feed you see by default on the Pinterest home page when you are logged in. One way to refine the feed is to unfollow specific boards from someone whose entire feed you were following. You also can unfollow individual boards even if you are not following a pinner's entire feed.

Unfollow a Board

1 On your profile page, click **Following**.

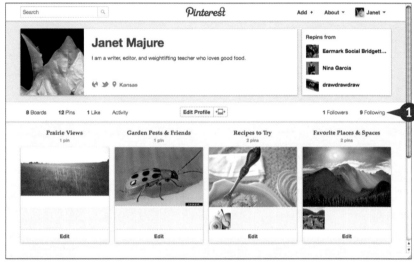

Pinterest displays all the pinners you are following.

2 Scroll down until you see the pinner whose board you want to unfollow.

3 Click the pinner's name or profile image.

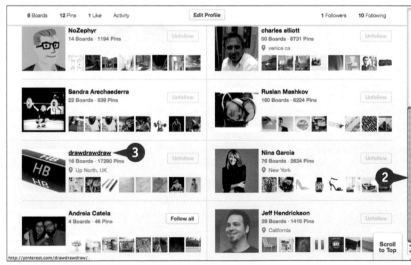

Pinterest displays the pinner's profile page.

4 Scroll down to review the boards.

5 If you see a board that you are not sure about, click the board name or image.

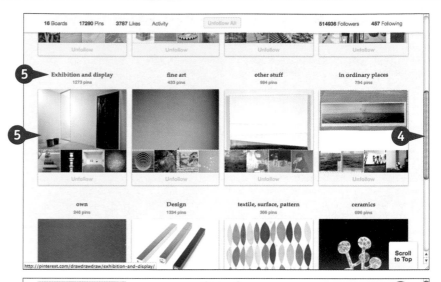

6 Scroll through the board to see what pins are there.

7 If you decide to quit following the board, click **Unfollow**.

The button changes to Follow.

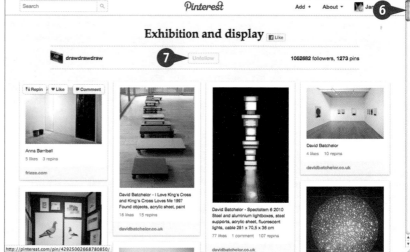

TIP

Is there a way to view the individual boards I am following separately from the pinners I am following?

Not at this time. Your profile page puts them both together under Following, with the profile images of the pinners displayed. When you are following a board or boards, rather than a pinner's entire feed, there will be a Follow All button beside the pinner. You need to go to the pinner's profile, where the board or boards you are following will display the Unfollow option.

Unlike a Pin

If you decide you do not want to accumulate endless likes or you fall out of like with an image that keeps appearing on a feed, you can trim your likes list. Maybe you just like to keep things neat. In any case, unliking is a simple process. First, you go to your Likes page, and then you click the Unlike button on the image you want to remove from the page.

Unlike a Pin

1 Click your name arrow and select **Likes** from the drop-down list.

A As an alternative, you can click Likes on your profile page.

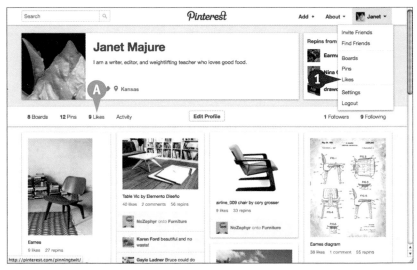

Your likes appear.

2 Scroll through the images until you see one you want to unlike.

3 Position your mouse ▶ over the image until the Repin, Unlike, and Comment buttons appear.

4 Click **Unlike**.

The Unlike button changes to Like, allowing you now to change your mind. Next time you show your likes, the image will be gone.

Note: As an alternative, you can click the image to see its pin page, position your pointer to reveal the Repin and Unlike buttons, and click the Unlike button.

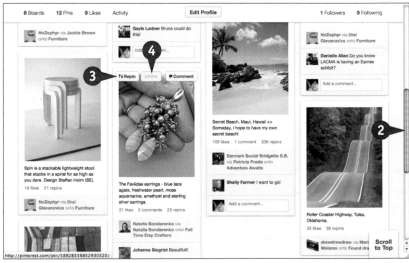

Delete a Comment You Made

If you have second thoughts about a comment you made, you can always delete it. You cannot edit your comment, but you can delete it and write a new one. The best place to focus on previous comments you made is in the Activity view of your profile page. Of course, if your second thoughts occur the moment you submit a comment, you can delete the comment immediately by clicking the image you commented on, which will take you to the pin's page. There, you can delete the comment.

Delete a Comment You Made

1 On your profile page, click **Activity**.

2 Scroll down until you find the comment you want to delete.

3 Click the image to open its pin page.

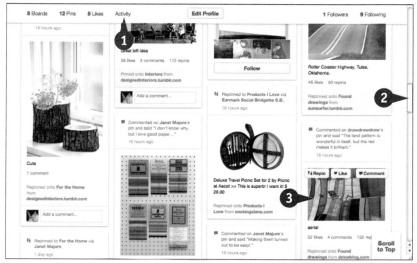

4 Scroll down to find your comment under the image.

5 Click the **X** to delete the comment.

The comment disappears.

Note: If you want to delete a brand new comment on a feed, just click the image in the feed. The pin page opens, where you can find your comment, and click the **X**.

Follow a Pin to Its Source

You can find out more about images you like by going to the source of the pin. When someone pins an image from a website, Pinterest automatically attaches source information to the pin. As a result, most times you can click an image on its pin page and arrive at the website where the image resides. That site likely provides additional information about the pin, such as information about where to buy an item, recipe details, or step-by-step craft instructions. Unfortunately, uploaded images and those pinned without following good practices may not always provide additional information.

Follow a Pin to Its Source

1 In a feed or profile page, click an image that interests you.

The image opens in a window superimposed over the page where you clicked.

2 Click the image.

Pinterest opens a new tab in your browser to the image's source.

Note: Your browser may open a new window instead.

A The article with the original image appears.

3 Scroll down to read the article.

4 Click the tab's **X** to close the tab.

The window closes, and the pin page reappears.

5 Position your mouse ![mouse pointer] over the image.

The Repin and Like buttons appear.

6 Click a button if you want to keep the image in your account.

7 Click the **Back** button (![back icon]) to return to the feed.

TIP

How can I get to the source if clicking the image does not reveal the origin?

If the image has been uploaded, you can leave a comment on the pin asking a question and then hope the pinner reads and responds. A more-frequent problem occurs when someone pins from the home page of a website that changes its home page often. In that case, clicking the pin takes you to the source's home page, but you see other images. You can try searching the site in hopes of finding the image, but there are no guarantees.

CHAPTER 3

Refining Your Pinterest Setup

The basic Pinterest setup works, but you can refine it to make it work in a way that better suits your needs. Refinement options include everything from how your profile appears to creating a group board.

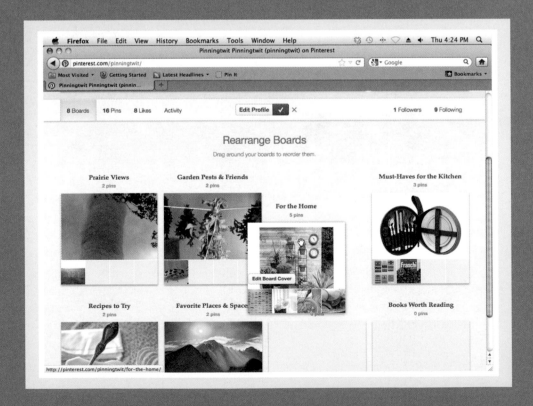

Understanding the Profile Page

Understanding your profile page will help you know which settings you may want to adjust. The profile page provides a sort of dashboard from which you can keep track of all your Pinterest boards, pins, follows, and other activity, including repins and comments. Your profile page is also the face that you present to the Pinterest community and the Internet world, so you may want to give careful consideration to what you display. You can always go to your profile page by clicking your name in the top-right corner of most Pinterest pages.

Ⓐ About You

Includes your name, a bio or description, and icons for your other connections on the web.

Ⓑ Repins

Highlights the last three pinners whose pins you have repinned and provides links to their profiles.

Ⓒ Information Bar

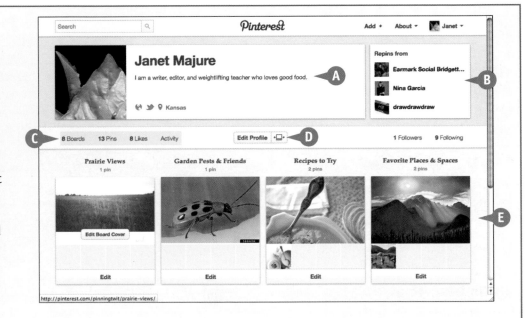

Shows statistics on boards, pins, likes, followers, and pinners who you are following; links to those features, your Activity page, and profile settings.

Ⓓ Rearrange Boards Button

Enables you to set the order in which boards appear on the page; visible only on the default/boards profile page.

Ⓔ Information Window, Default Display

Shows your boards as the default display, and provides links to display pins, likes, your Pinterest activity, who is following you, and who you are following.

Ⓐ Information Window, Pins Display

Shows your pins and repins, with your most recent pin at the top left. Clicking an image opens its pin page.

Ⓑ Pin Description

Includes the description you recorded when pinning plus comments and repinning counts, if pertinent.

Ⓒ Source and Destination

Identifies the source of the original pin and the board where you pinned it.

Ⓓ Comments

Shows comments made on your pin, but not on the original pin.

Ⓐ Information Windows, Likes Display

Shows images you like with the most recent one first. Clicking the image opens its pin page.

Ⓑ Pin Description

Shows the pinner's description of the pin plus counts of likes, comments, and repins, if pertinent.

Ⓒ Pinner Information

Shows who pinned the image you liked, the board where he placed it, and, if it is a repin, the original pinner.

Ⓓ Comments

Lists comments on the pin or repin that you liked.

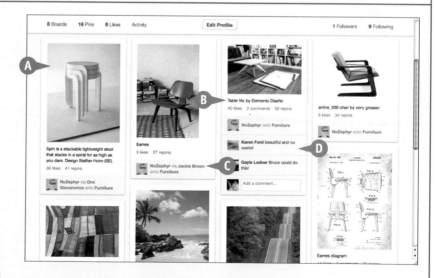

Change the Information About You

You can change the information about you that appears on your profile page. Perhaps you did not realize when you signed up which information would appear publicly. Maybe you want your username, rather than your real name, on view to give you a measure of privacy. Alternatively, perhaps you want your username to be the same as your real name for business purposes or to increase your brand identity. Both options are available when you edit your profile, and you can add or change other information, too.

Change the Information About You

1 Click your name.

Your profile page opens.

2 Click **Edit Profile**.

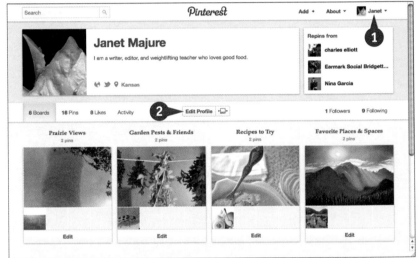

The Edit Profile page opens.

3 Type a name in the First name box.

Note: Your username is a convenient choice.

4 Type the rest of the public name you want in the Last name box.

Note: You must have something in both boxes.

5 If you want to change your username, type a new one.

Note: It must be 3 to 15 characters long.

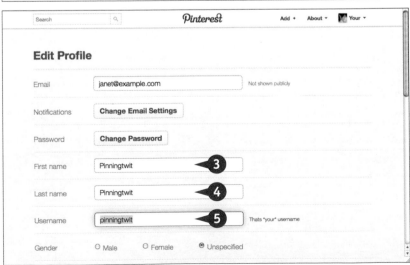

6 Scroll down to reveal the About box.

7 Type the description or bio you want publicly associated with your account.

8 Review your location, website, and image and make changes if desired.

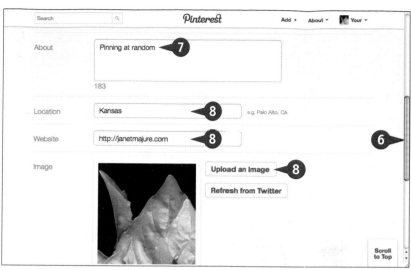

9 Scroll to the bottom of the screen.

10 Click **Save Profile**.

Pinterest returns to your profile page, where your new information appears.

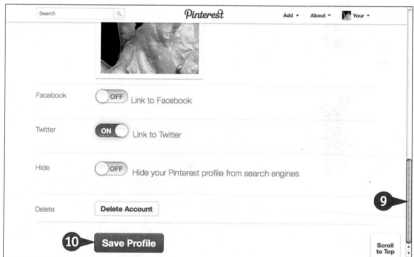

TIPS

If I change my username, am I creating a new account?
No. The only thing that changes is your URL for your profile page. You keep the same social media connections, your pins, and everything else associated with the original username.

If I change my name, does the change apply only to my profile page?
No. Your name, not your username, is what people see on your profile page and next to your pins. If you change your name, all previous and future pins or repins will show the new name. If you want people to see your username next to your pins, you can turn your username into your name, keeping in mind that your username is a single word and your name needs to have a first and last name.

Adjust Your E-mail Settings

You can choose where you get Pinterest e-mail messages, and you can choose what kind of messages you receive. The default setting is for Pinterest to send you an e-mail every time someone follows you, likes a pin, or repins a pin. That may be more e-mail than you want, or it may make it more fun. It all depends on your preferences. Fortunately, Pinterest understands and gives you a long list of options, including how often you get e-mail messages. It just takes a few clicks to set your options.

Adjust Your E-mail Settings

1 Position the mouse ⬆ over your name at the top of a Pinterest page.

A drop-down list appears.

2 Click **Settings**.

The Edit Profile page opens.

3 Click **Change Email Settings**.

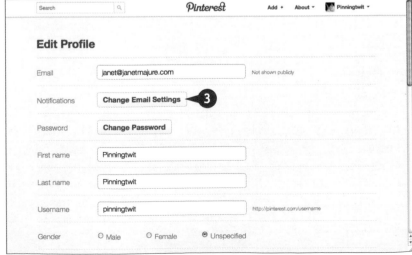

The Email Settings page opens. The default for all settings is *On*.

④ Click the **On** toggle next to the e-mail option you want to change. (On changes to Off.)

Note: Clicking the setting description, such as When someone likes your pin, also toggles the On-Off setting.

⑤ Scroll to the bottom of the page.

⑥ Click any **On-Off** settings you want to change.

⑦ Select a **Frequency** setting option (○ changes to ⊙).

⑧ Click **Save Settings**.

Pinterest saves your selections and returns to the top of the page.

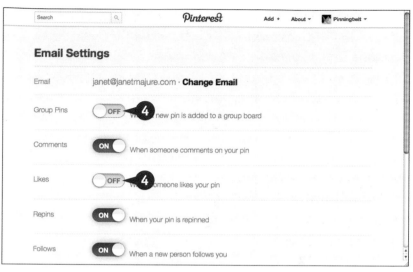

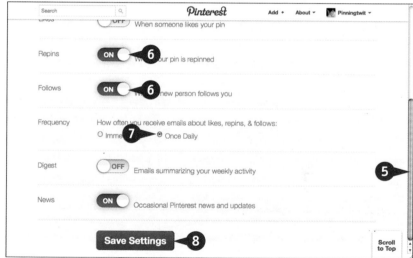

How can I change my e-mail address?
To change your e-mail address, follow Steps **1** to **2** in this section. On the Edit Profile page, simply type a new address in the Email box. Next, scroll to the bottom of the page and click **Save Profile**.

Why am I still receiving e-mail at my old address after clicking the Change Email option at the top of the Email Settings page?
You probably forgot to scroll to the bottom of the Edit Profile page to click **Save Profile**. Go back to the **Edit Profile** page. Chances are it shows your old address. Reenter the new address, scroll to the bottom of the page, and click **Save Profile**.

Rename a Board

You can set yourself apart from the pinning masses and probably make things easier to find if you give your boards personal and descriptive names. Many people have identically named boards, a result of the way Pinterest used to initiate members. Those boards' titles tend to be very broad. It might be easier to find that fabulous chair — and draw more followers — if you pinned it to Fabulous Furniture of the Future rather than, ho-hum, For the Home. To change any boring board names you have, you can rename them on the Edit Board page.

Rename a Board

1 Click your name.

Your profile page opens.

2 Click the board name you want to change.

Your board page appears, showing its pins.

3 Click **Edit Board**.

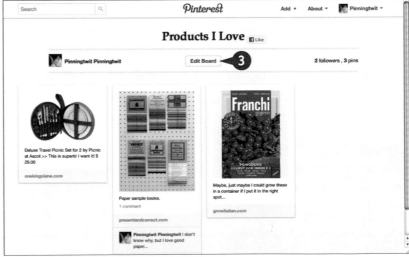

The Edit Board/*board title* page opens, where *board title* is the current title of the board.

4 Type a new name in the Title box.

5 Type a description.

6 Click **Save Settings**.

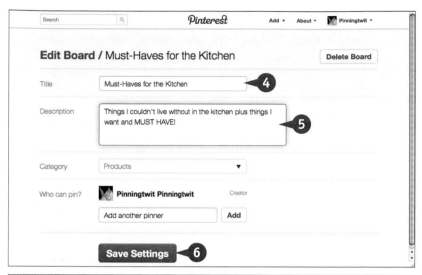

Your board page reopens.

A The board displays its new title.

B The new description appears below the title.

7 Click your name.

Pinterest returns to your profile page.

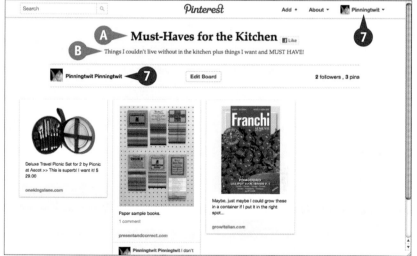

TIPS

Do I have to rename my board titles, or can I use the standard boards that Pinterest suggested when I signed up?
It depends on whether you want other people to find and follow you. If you want followers, a more descriptive board title allows more people to find it by searching. If the title is amusing or provokes people's curiosity, they might click through on a pin to see what else is there.

Is there a limit on how long the pinboard titles are?
Yes. Pinterest limits pinboard titles to 180 characters. A short title is probably better anyway, because a long title does not look good when it appears under pinned images.

Rearrange Your Boards

You can rearrange your boards as you see fit. You do not have to accept the order in which your pinboards appear on your profile page. If you take no action, the last board you create is the first one you and others see. If you like, you can put your boards in alphabetical order or organize them by categories. For example, you could cluster activity-related boards in one group, products in another, and pretty things in yet another. Organizing the boards is a simple matter of dragging them on your screen to where you want them to be.

Rearrange Your Boards

1 Click your name.

Your profile page opens.

2 Click the **Rearrange Boards** icon (⊡).

A A red check mark appears (✓).

B Pinterest tells you how to move boards.

3 Click and drag a board from one position to a new position on your page.

C The board slides into its new position, and the board previously at the end of that row shifts to the next row.

④ Click and drag another board to a new location.

The board slides into position, and Pinterest shifts other boards to fill the gap.

⑤ When you are satisfied with your arrangement, click ✔.

Pinterest saves the arrangement, and the rearranging instructions disappear.

Ⓓ The Save Arrangement message appears momentarily.

Ⓔ The Edit Profile check mark (✔) appears and it changes to the Rearrange Boards icon (⊡).

TIPS

Is there a way to mark boards to rearrange them as a group?

No. You must click and drag each board individually. You may find it helpful to put your boards in the desired order every time you add one board. Doing so will prevent the need to rearrange them all at once.

Is there a more efficient way to rearrange a large number of boards, given that this way does not let me see more than a few boards at a time?

If you are having difficulty rearranging a large number of boards, remembering the way boards shift can be helpful. For example, if you move a board to the row above it, the board at the end of the new line becomes the first board in the next line.

Set Your Board Cover Image

The *board cover image* is the big picture at the top of your board. By choosing a meaningful board cover image, you and your followers can tell at a glance what your pinboard is all about. In combination with a good title, a snappy cover image also can attract followers. If you do not set a board cover image, Pinterest automatically displays your latest pin as the board cover. You can fix that in no time by clicking your name and going to your profile page, where you can set your board cover image.

Set Your Board Cover Image

① Position the mouse ⬉ over the board whose cover image you want to set.

The Edit Board Cover button appears.

② Click **Edit Board Cover**.

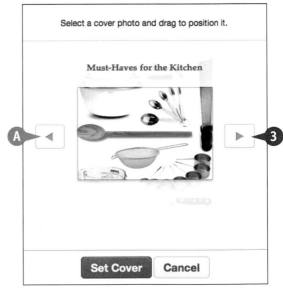

The Set Cover window opens.

③ Click the right arrow (▶) to find the image you want.

Images from the pinboard rotate into view.

Ⓐ Click the left arrow (◀) to reverse direction.

B The horizontal rectangle shows the portion of the image that appears as the board cover.

C Parts of the image that fall outside the board cover are dimmed.

4 Click any part of the image and drag until the portion of the image you want as your board cover appears in the horizontal rectangle.

5 When you are satisfied, click **Set Cover**.

D The window slips away, and the board reappears with its new cover.

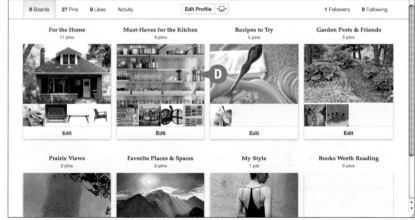

TIPS

Can I change the proportions of the board cover image to make it square or vertical?
No. The tip cover shape is preset. Your only option is choosing what part of a vertical or square image appears when you drag the selection box in the Set Cover window.

Is there an alternative way to set the board cover image?
You can open the board first by clicking the board's name on your profile page. Then you can scroll through all the board's pins. Position your mouse ▶ over the image you want as the board cover; the Set Board Cover button appears. Click it, and that image becomes the first visible one in the Set Cover window.

Hide Comments from Feeds

You can make it easier to scan images when you choose to hide comments from feeds. Perhaps you do not find the comments helpful, or perhaps the comments get in the way of your visual review of pins, and pictures is what Pinterest is all about. Happily, a fellow by the name of Craig Fifield has created a bookmarklet that lets you toggle comments on and off as you view Pinterest feeds. For more information on installing a bookmarklet, see Chapter 1.

Hide Comments from Feeds

1 In your browser's address bar, type **www.craigfifield.com/pinterest-bookmarklet.htm** and press **Enter** (**Return**).

2 Scroll down until you see the Toggle Pinterest Comments link.

3 Click and drag the link to your browser's bookmark bar.

4 Release the mouse button.

The link sticks to the bookmarks bar.

5 In your browser's address bar, type **pinterest.com/popular** and press **Enter** (**Return**), or type another active Pinterest feed.

A Note the numerous comments and the visibility of five images.

6 Click the **Toggle Pinterest** bookmarklet.

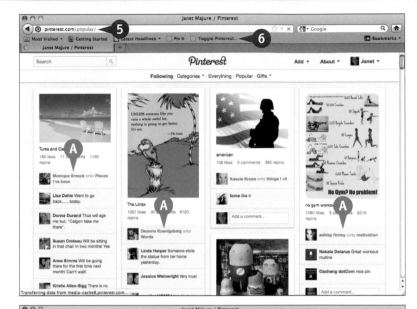

The comments disappear.

B Note the absence of comments and the visibility of at least seven images.

7 Click the **Toggle Pinterest** bookmarklet to return the comments to view.

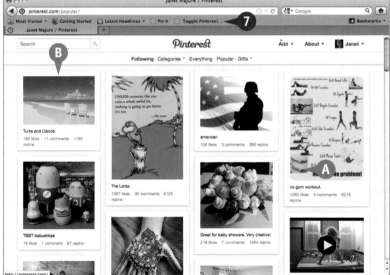

TIP

Why do the comments reappear when I go to another feed?

The toggle works on a page at a time as you are viewing the page. When you go to another page, you need to click the bookmarklet again if you want to hide the comments. In fact, if you hide comments, go to another feed, and then click your browser's **Back** button ◀, you will need to click the bookmarklet again to hide the comments again.

CHAPTER 4

Building Your Community

One of the great things about Pinterest is that you can build a community based on your interests. Whether those interests are as commonplace as a need for easy recipes or as obscure as a passion for opossums, you will find companions on Pinterest.

Make a Pinning Plan

Y ou can develop a basic pinning plan that will help you find the images you want, the people you want to follow, and the people you hope will follow you. Pinterest is so appealing that it is tempting and easy to jump in without forethought. The trouble is you may wind up with a muddled mass of images and discover that you have spent hours on Pinterest without getting organized.

Think About Your Pinterest Goals

You can use Pinterest for anything from passing the time while you wait at the doctor's office to organizing a major business presentation. Before you start your Pinterest plan, spend a few minutes determining what you want out of Pinterest. Maybe you simply want to keep up with your friends' favorite recipes, but perhaps you want to create an online following that you can use to promote your organization. Most likely you will be headed somewhere in between, and your goals may evolve. Still, identifying what you want out of your initial Pinterest activities can save you many wasted hours online.

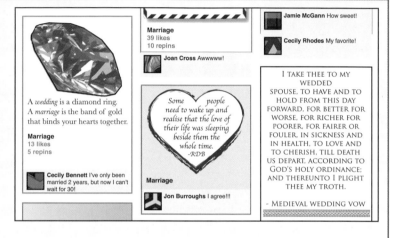

Start with a Few Topics

Think about subjects that hold your interest, whether they are things you love or make you laugh, people you adore, places you have been or want to visit, problems that you are trying to solve, or goals that you want to achieve. Make a list of them and narrow the list to a half-dozen or so topics. Start with those topics as the basis for your pins, repins, boards, and follows. Having those topics in mind will make your pinning more useful both to you and to others in the Pinterest community.

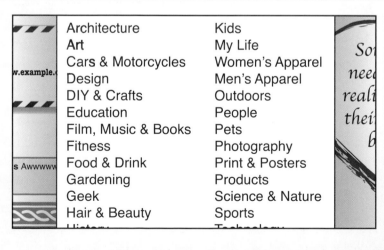

Create Boards for Your Topics

Once you know your topics, create new boards, or rename your existing boards to closely reflect the subject matter. The more descriptive and colorful the board names, the more likely you are to remember what goes where and the more likely others with your interests will find your boards. If you want to remodel your bathroom, make a Small Bathroom Remodeling Ideas board, rather than one labeled simply Remodeling or Bathroom. Likewise, go for Teacher Retirement Party Plans instead of a generic Party Planning board.

Create a Board

Be a Giver, Not Just a Taker

The easiest approach to pinning is to scroll through Pinterest images and then repin the images to your boards. That is fine, but more people will find you — and thereby allow you to find them — if in addition you contribute to the Pinterest image pool by pinning from elsewhere on the web and uploading your own images. The most popular pinners post numerous original pins. Plan to follow their example by checking out your favorite websites, or click through to the source on favorite Pinterest images to find more images you want to add to Pinterest.

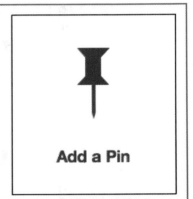

Add a Pin

Choose a Following Plan

Besides planning your boards and your pins, you need to plan who to follow. It matters who you follow, because their images are the ones that will appear by default when you log on to Pinterest. You can follow friends, family, popular pinners, people whose interests you share, or businesses to which you are loyal. You could follow any or all of

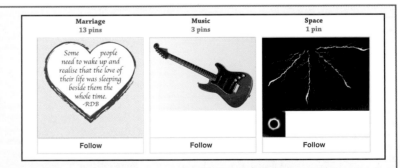

them, but if you make a point to follow people whose pins fit with your Pinterest goals and topics, you probably will find your Pinterest time is more satisfying.

Follow and Invite Facebook Friends

If you want your friends to be a highlight of your Pinterest community, then you can invite them in a hurry by using Facebook. Pinterest displays not only a list of your Facebook friends already on Pinterest — you can follow them with just a click — but it also displays all your other Facebook friends, making it easy for you to send invitations to them. Many people like the way Pinterest encourages them to connect with their friends based on their interests rather than on the drama and mundane concerns in their daily lives.

Follow and Invite Facebook Friends

Follow Facebook Friends

1 Position your mouse ▶ over your name.

Your account menu opens.

2 Click **Find Friends**.

Ⓐ If your account is connected with Facebook, as an alternative you can click **See All**.

Pinterest opens a new page.

3 Click **Follow** beside any friends on Pinterest who you would like to follow.

The Follow button changes to Unfollow.

4 Scroll down to see more Facebook friends who also are on Pinterest, and choose ones to follow.

Ⓑ If you want to follow all your Facebook friends who are Pinterest members, click **Follow All**.

Invite Facebook Friends to Join Pinterest

5 Under Invite Friends, click **Invite** beside the names of friends you would like to join Pinterest.

The Invite button dims and after a moment, a Facebook message window opens.

Note: You can click multiple Invites, and a separate message window opens for each.

6 Type a message in the message box.

7 Click **Send**.

C Your message from Pinterest goes to your friend's Messages list on Facebook.

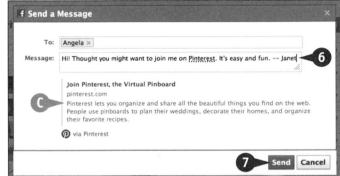

TIP

Does Pinterest have any tools to help me sort out my long friends list?

Pinterest helps in two ways. If you start typing the name of a friend in the search box under Invite Friends, Pinterest will show only friends with the letters you type. At the bottom of the Friends on Pinterest list is a link that reads Already following *n* friends, where *n* is the number of Facebook friends you are following. Click that link, and Pinterest shows the friends you are following.

Follow Friends Through Yahoo

You can add to those friends you are following if you keep a contact list on Yahoo. The Yahoo connection is handy for Pinterest users who do not use Facebook — whether that might be you *or* your friends. The Yahoo friends page provides an easy way for you to follow your Yahoo contacts who are on Pinterest. At this writing, however, it does not provide a simple way to *invite* your Yahoo contacts, even though an Invite Friends box appears. Watch for the functionality in the future.

Follow Friends Through Yahoo

1 Position your mouse ➤ over your name.

Your account menu opens.

2 Click **Invite Friends**.

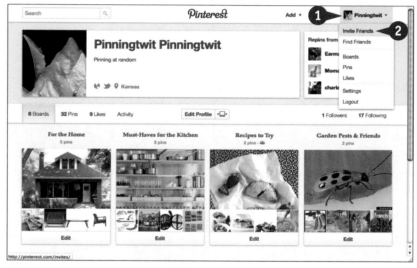

The Invites page opens.

3 Click **Yahoo**.

The page changes and presents a large button reading *Find Friends from Yahoo*.

4 Click the **Find Friends from Yahoo** button.

An authorization window
pops up.

5 Click **Agree** to authorize the
connection.

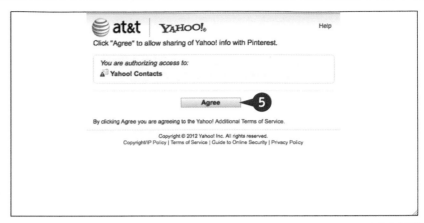

Pinterest loads your Yahoo
contacts, which may take a
minute.

6 Click **Follow** next to contacts
you want to follow in
Pinterest.

Follow changes to Unfollow.

A If you prefer, you can click
Follow All to follow all your
Yahoo contacts that are on
Pinterest.

TIPS

Is there a way to see what my friends' boards are like before I decide to follow them?
Yes. You can go to a friend's profile page from the Yahoo friends page, where it lists contacts on Pinterest. Simply click the friend's name or profile image. Pinterest takes you to that friend's profile page. Click your browser's **Back** button (🔙) to return to your Yahoo friends.

Will my friends know I am following them?
Yes. Pinterest sends each friend an e-mail telling the friend that you are following her. The notification she receives gives your name as it appears on your Settings page, also known as the Edit Profile page.

Invite Friends Through E-mail

Simply typing in e-mail addresses is another way you can invite friends to join Pinterest and is especially useful for friends who are not on Facebook. E-mail also is the quickest way to send a single invitation or two to your friends or relatives. You can send up to four e-mail invitations at a time. By sending invitations through e-mail, you are not sharing your entire contacts list with Pinterest, if that bothers you. The disadvantage is more typing is involved.

Invite Friends Through E-mail

1 Position your mouse ▸ over your name.

Your account menu opens.

2 Click **Invite Friends**.

The Invites page opens.

3 Click **Email**.

The Invite Your Friends to Pinterest page appears.

④ Type one or more e-mail addresses.

⑤ Type a message in the box.

⑥ Click **Send Invites**.

Pinterest sends invitations to the addresses you provided.

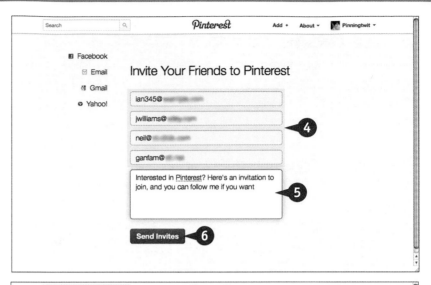

Ⓐ Pinterest displays a confirmation message for each successful send operation.

TIPS

Can I use the Gmail link on the Invites page to invite my friends?

Yes, if you click the Gmail link, Pinterest lists Gmail contacts you can invite, and it lists Gmail contacts already on Pinterest. To invite a contact, click the person's name. A dialog box appears with the person's e-mail address. You add a message and click **Invite**, and Pinterest sends a message to your contact.

Can I put multiple e-mail addresses in one box, separating them with semicolons or something similar?

No. Pinterest is designed for just one address per box. If you put in more than one address, Pinterest tells you that your entry does not appear to be a valid e-mail address. This is true even if you separate the addresses with a semicolon or comma, as you might in an e-mail program.

Alert a Pinner to a Pin

You can let a person know about a pin, repin, or comment that you make, and you can make it happen while you are creating the pin, repin, or comment. You just need to know the person's name, not the username, and precede it with the @ symbol in a pin description or comment. Pinterest then alerts that person by way of an e-mail message that you have mentioned him. Using the @ symbol also creates a live link that lets other people simply click your friend's name to go to his profile page.

Alert a Pinner to a Pin

1 On a page with an image that you want to pin, click the **Pin It** bookmarklet button.

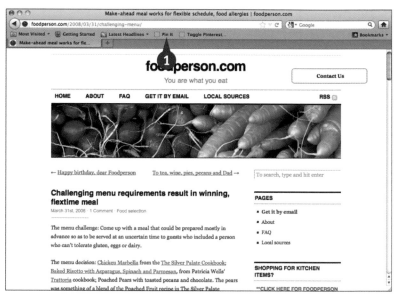

The Create Pin window opens.

2 Type a description in the box, followed by the @ symbol, and the first few letters of a friend's name.

Pinterest shows possible friends to notify based on the characters you type.

3 Click the name of the friend you want to notify.

4 Click the **Board** down arrow (▼) and select a board from the drop-down list.

5 When you are finished with your description, click **Pin It**.

Pinterest sends an e-mail notice to your friend, and the bookmarklet shows a Success message.

6 Click **See your Pin**.

Pinterest opens your pin in the pin window.

Ⓐ The pin appears with your friend's name in bold and as an active link. Other viewers can click the name to see the friend's profile page.

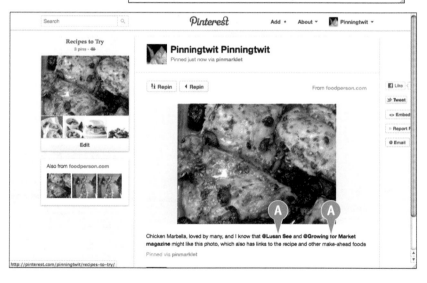

TIPS

Does this technique work only on new pins when I create them with the bookmarklet?
No. You can use the same technique when you repin at Pinterest or when you make a new pin using the Add+ button on the Pinterest menu bar. You also can add an alert by editing the description of an existing pin on your board.

How do I create an alert in a comment?
To create an alert in a comment that you are writing under an image, type @ followed by a few letters and then click the name of your friend from the list that appears. When you are finished with your comment, click **Comment**. The comment appears under the image, and your friend receives a notice.

Add Hashtags to an Image

Adding *hashtags*, or active keywords, to your pins, repins, and comments provides another means by which people can find your contributions and related contributions to a particular topic. When you add a hashtag, the pin or comment produces a live link to a search page. The page provides the same results as if you typed the term associated with the hashtag into the Pinterest search box. You can add multiple hashtags to create more search options. However, you cannot do multiple-word hashtags.

Add Hashtags to an Image

1 Position your mouse ▸ over the image you want to repin.

The Repin button appears.

2 Click **Repin**.

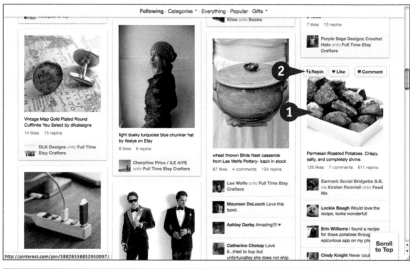

The Repin window opens.

3 Type **#** and a keyword in your description.

Note: You can include multiple hashtags.

4 Click the down arrow (▾) and select a board from the drop-down list.

5 Click **Pin It**.

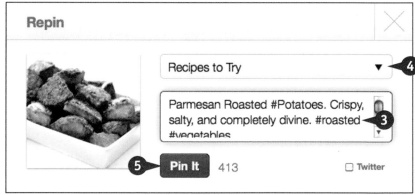

Pinterest adds the image to your page and briefly shows a confirmation message.

6 Click **See it now** (not shown).

The image appears on its pin page.

A Your description, with hashtags, appears below the image.

7 Position your mouse ↖ over a hashtag, and click the hashtag when it turns red.

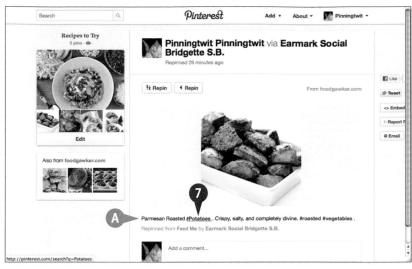

A search page based on the hashtag term opens.

B Images with the hashtag appear in a feed.

C You can click these options to see boards or people associated with the hashtag term.

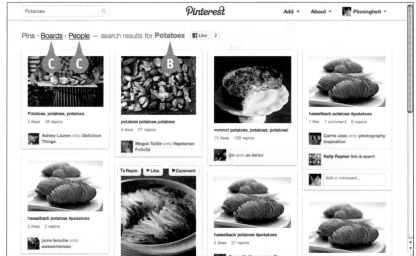

TIP

Are there any rules as to what kind of words to put in hashtags?

Aim to use words that would help you and others find the image. Hashtags that are more specific are useful to people seeking specific subjects. For instance, *heron* may be more helpful than *bird*, but you could include both to help pinners interested in all birds as well as those interested specifically in herons. Avoid using more than a few hashtags at a time, as too many hashtags look like spam.

Follow Pinners Who Repin Your Pins

A great way to build community among your fellow pinners is to follow people who repin your pins. You know they share at least some of your interests based on their decision to repin your pins. Pinterest tells you by e-mail when someone has repinned your pins unless you have turned off such notices. It also shows you on the Pinterest home page recent repins of your pin. You can follow these pinners from your Pinterest home page.

Follow Pinners Who Repin Your Pins

1 Find repin reports in the Recent Activity box on your Pinterest home page.

2 Click a repin report.

Note: You can click the thumbnail or the activity description.

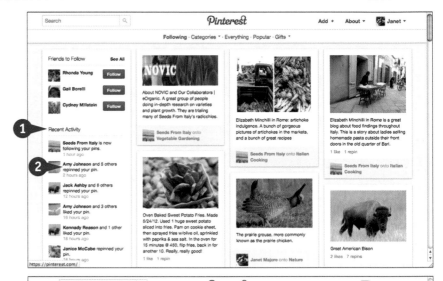

The page associated with that pin opens.

3 Scroll down to see the list of repins.

4 Click the name of a repinner.

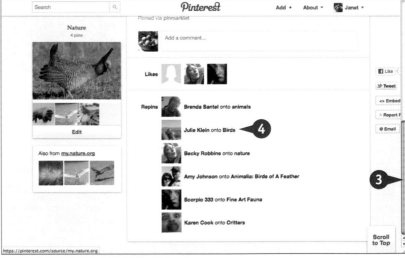

5 Click **Follow** under a board.

A As an alternative, you can click **Follow All** if you want to follow all of that pinner's boards.

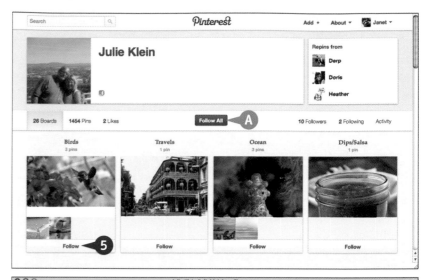

B When Follow changes to Unfollow, you are following the pinner's board.

6 Click the browser's **Back** button (◀).

Pinterest returns to the pin's page, where you can consider other pinners to follow.

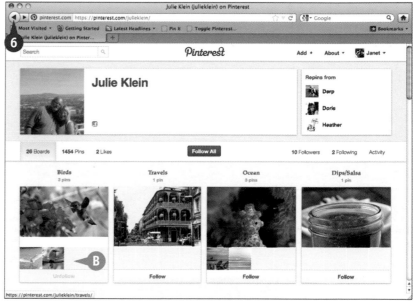

TIP

Is it better to follow a pinner or follow a board?
You may see a pinner with a few interesting boards and not very many pins and decide to follow all of them. If a pinner has 47 boards and 11,438 pins, however, you might be better off choosing one or a few select boards. Following all boards of one very active pinner can result in that pinner dominating the default Pinners You Follow feed.

E-mail a Pin

You can e-mail a pin to someone who is not a Pinterest member. Doing so is a great way to share with your nonmember friends your finds while on Pinterest as well as to encourage them to join you. The first step is to find an image that you want to pass on to a friend. The image could be on a feed or a board. Then, you need to have your friend's e-mail address handy to type into the e-mail window, which also gives you the option to add a personal message.

E-mail a Pin

1 Click the image you want to e-mail.

The pin's page opens.

2 Click @ **Email**.

The Email This Pin window opens.

3 Type your friend's name.

4 Type the friend's e-mail address.

5 Type a message if you like.

6 Click **Send Email**.

Email This Pin

3 — Lynn

4 — lynn@example.com

5 — I don't know if this spot is on your itinerary, but you need to add it!

6 — **Send Email**

The Send Email button briefly changes to Sending, and then to Sent.

Email This Pin

Lynn

lynn@example.com

I don't know if this spot is on your itinerary, but you need to add it!

Sending...

When I tried to e-mail a pin, the Send Email window switched to Sending and got stuck there. Did I do something wrong?

You probably tried to send it during a heavy-traffic time for Pinterest. As the website experiences growing pains, its servers become overloaded and delay the processing of everything from sending e-mail messages to updating your feed. Your best solution probably is to click the image's **Like** button or save it to one of your boards. Then, go back later and try again to e-mail the pin.

Make Yourself Worth Following

You can do a lot to make yourself someone who people value on Pinterest. Choosing beautiful and interesting images is only the beginning. Exercising good habits as you pin will go far in your efforts to build good relationships with other people on Pinterest. Those habits include keeping the Pinterest etiquette in mind, and providing useful information as you pin. Useful information includes descriptive terms in the description and making sure your source goes to an exact location rather than to a general website.

Always Include Descriptions

When you are on a roll adding images to your Pinterest boards, you may be tempted to pin now, describe later. Resist the urge. Be sure to include at least a brief description of the image. Doing so helps you and others conduct searches. It also helps later when you may wonder why you pinned a particular image. Many times, some kind of description will appear automatically in the box. Go ahead and note why this pin is worth keeping for *you*. Write something like, *This room design could work for the guest room*, rather than simply *interesting room*.

Description	A John Hulsey painting from Rocky Mountain National Park.

Keep Descriptions Brief and Useful

As essential as descriptions are, remember that less is more when it comes to the *length* of your description. Although Pinterest allows up to 500 words in the description, users are likely to skip over long text. Instead, simply try to answer the immediate questions a viewer might have. For instance, you might say when and where a landscape image was taken or mention that the potato salad pictured is the best you have ever eaten. Remember that the essence of Pinterest is visual. If you want to wax poetic about an image, do it in another forum and add a link to your essay.

Quinoa Black Bean Burrito Bowl. This sounds so good and fresh... >> Yum! #vegetarian

Repinned onto **Recipes to Try** from **theshiksa.com**

Pin from the Primary Source

Some websites, particularly blogs and magazine-type sites, display images on their home pages, but those images change regularly. If you are pinning from such a site, before you select the URL or use the Pin It bookmarklet, try clicking the image to see if it takes you to an individual article or blog post. If it does, use that URL or click the bookmarklet from that location. If you do it from the site's home page, there is a good chance that a person on Pinterest is not going to find the original image if she later clicks your pin in hopes of seeing it at its source.

Egypt Finally Sheds Notorious Law

MORE WORLD ▶ **Wickedest City On Earth.. Police Raid Brothels.. Ancient Roman Shipwrecks.. U.S. Tourists Kidnapped**

Comments | ⊕ Hosni Mubarak

Use Good and Big Images

To be a good contributing member of Pinterest, make sure your images are worth looking at. You also might want to make sure the images are big enough. Pinterest does not limit how big an image can be, but it does not allow images smaller than 81 pixels in any direction. *Pixel* is a digital image measurement based on the tiny colored dots that make up images on a computer display. If you are uploading images, you might be interested to know that the pin page displays images 554 pixels wide. Smaller images have white space around them.

240 px wide

554 px wide

Do Comment, but Be Judicious

It is fun to receive and read comments about your pins, and other pinners will appreciate your comments too — unless you get carried away. Compliments are nice, but even better are comments that extend the conversation. For example, if you see an image from a place you visited, you might tell viewers about other interesting sights there. Questions also are good. If you see a sofa that you have been looking for, ask where you can see or buy that sofa. If you post too many comments, though, particularly in a short amount of time, you might be identified as a possible spammer and temporarily locked out. See Chapter 11 for help.

Traci Rutledge
My family loves this! The chicken is so tender and yummy!

Kristina Marie
This may be a stupid question but I have to ask (I am new to the crockpot world). Can I place the chicken breasts on top of each other in the crock pot or do they have to be side by side in 1 single layer and not over-lapping? I would really like to try this recipe.

Traci Rutledge
Kristina- I just pile 'em in there and they cook just fine! Good luck!

CHAPTER 5

Curating Your Boards

Curating your boards means organizing their content. When you do a good job of curating, you will find it easier to pin, to find the images you have pinned, and to attract followers who share your interests.

Create a Boards Plan

Just as planning your pins makes for more satisfying pinning, planning your boards makes for more successful boards. You will develop your own definition of a successful board, but at this stage, think of a successful board as one where you and others know its contents at a glance. A clear name for it lets you make a quick board choice when you are pinning images. This section assumes you already have plans for what kind of pinning you will do.

Determine How Many Boards Are Enough

There is no right or wrong number of boards, but the number definitely is something to consider. If your interests are narrow and few, you most likely will be content with a handful of boards. With just four boards, you can see all of them at the same time without having to scroll on your profile page. With eight, you can see all your boards at once by scrolling or paging down. Having fewer boards also makes it easier when you are pinning, as you will have only a small number to choose from in the drop-down list. However, if your boards are few, it is easy to wind up with a disorganized bunch of pins.

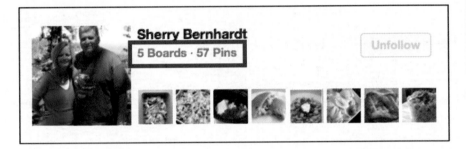

Consider How Many Boards Are Too Many

When you have more than eight boards, you must scroll down to see them, and when you post a pin, you will have to scroll through a long list to choose a board to pin it to. You may also wind up with duplicates if you are not careful. One pinner, for example, has Full Time Etsy Crafters, Artisan Galley of Etsy, Etsy Awesomeness, and Incredible Etsy finds. Perhaps she can distinguish among the four, but it is unlikely other people can.

Use a Decision Tree for Organizing

You may have trouble dividing your pins into boards. One approach is to create a *decision tree*, where each branch requires a decision that leads you to a single choice. For example, you could divide the first branch among people, places, and things. Then, you might have

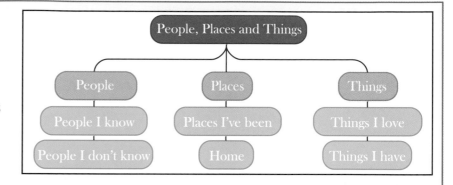

people you know and people you do not know; places you have visited, places you want to visit, and home; and for things, you might pin things you admire but do not want, things you want, and things you have. Try this approach using branches that pertain to your interests.

Decide Who Will Contribute

You can keep your boards as your own creations, or you can invite other Pinterest members to contribute. By default, boards are yours alone, but you can get more pins and more dynamic activity on your boards when other people augment your pinning efforts. Having contributors, though, has its drawbacks, as discussed later in this chapter. If you see a board with a curious-looking icon next to the number of pins on the profile page of someone you follow, it probably is a group board. Take a look, and see how groups work for other pinners.

Consider the Layout of Your Boards

You can rearrange your boards on your profile page. Although the arrangement is easier to change than, say, your decision tree hierarchy, it is easier to navigate your boards page if you have a logical layout. You could sort boards alphabetically, which makes sense if your board names

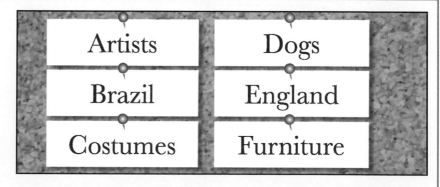

are single words, such as Cats. You could organize them in related groups, which is helpful when you have more boards. Using the example of people, places, and things, you could put all your things boards next to one another, and group your places and people similarly.

Categorize Your Boards

When you categorize your boards, your pins to those boards may show up on Pinterest feeds when people use categories to view images. By setting categories, you also make sure that you are the one who decides what categories fit your boards. You may not realize that you could have created boards without associating them with a category. If you do not categorize them, you not only limit the ways people can find your boards but you also leave yourself open to other people choosing the category for you.

Categorize Your Boards

1 Click your name.

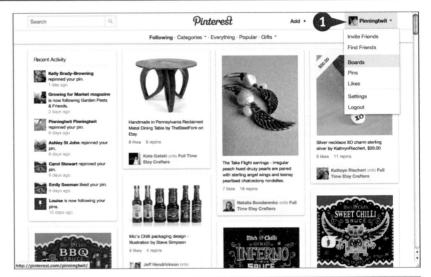

The profile page appears, with your boards as the default view.

2 Click your first board's cover image.

The board's display page opens.

Ⓐ If your board has no category, a banner appears at the top of the board's page telling you so.

❸ Click the **Select a Category** arrow (⬍).

❹ Select the category you want from the drop-down list.

The no-category banner disappears, and a confirmation message appears in its place.

❺ If you are satisfied with your selection, click **Close**.

Note: If you are not satisfied, click **Undo**, and the banner reappears with the Select a Category menu.

❻ Click the **Back** button (◀) on your browser or click your name to return to your profile page.

❼ Repeat Steps **2** to **6** for each board.

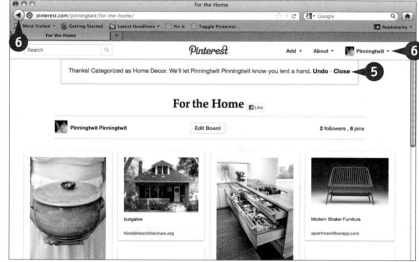

TIP

How do I find out what category a board is in if the board does not have a category reminder banner?
Click the board on your profile page, which opens the board's page. Then, click the **Edit Board** button on the board's page. When you do, it opens the Edit Board screen and displays the selected category. It is a good policy to check each board's category, because people frequently forget to set categories when they create boards. Generally, the result is that the new board gets assigned to the last board category you used.

Move a Pin to a Different Board

Y̶ou can move a pin from one board to another if you make a mistake while pinning it or if you simply change your mind about where you want that image to go. You also may want to move a pin if you want to split a board's images between two boards or, conversely, to merge one board with another. As you curate your boards' content, the desire to move a pin is sure to arise. Start by going to your profile page and its default boards view by clicking your name at the top of the window.

Move a Pin to a Different Board

1 Click the cover image or board name of the board you want to review.

The board's page opens.

2 Scroll to review the board's images.

3 When you see a pin you want to move, position your mouse ▸ over the image until buttons appear at the top of the image.

4 Click **Edit**.

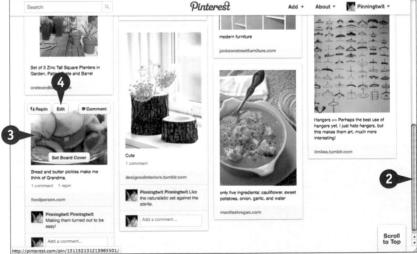

The Edit Pin window opens.

5 Click the board name to open the Board drop-down list.

6 Select the board where you want to move the pin.

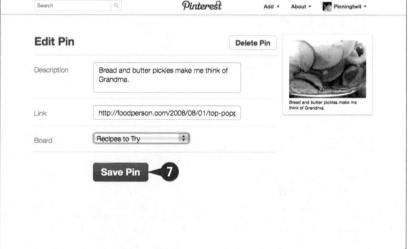

Your selection appears in the Board box.

7 Click **Save Pin**.

Pinterest saves the pin's new category and opens the pin's page, which displays the board to which the image is pinned.

TIP

Can I move a pin to two boards at one time, or move a group of pins from one board to another?
If you move a pin twice, it stays at the last board you moved it to. Instead, try moving the pin to one board and then repinning it to a second board. To do so, use the Repin button that appears when you position your mouse ▶ over the image on the board's page or the pin's page. At this time, however, you cannot move groups of pins. They must be moved individually.

Delete a Pin from a Board

Y ou can delete a pin from a board if you change your mind about the image or decide you simply do not need it anymore. This can happen, for example, if you are planning an event and you rule out an item or two on your party-planning board. Keep in mind, however, that deleting a pin from your board deletes the pin entirely from your account; you cannot keep images that are not pinned to a board. Begin by clicking your name at the top of a Pinterest window to go to your profile page in the default boards view.

Delete a Pin from a Board

1 Click the cover image or board name of the board you want to review.

The board's page opens.

2 Scroll to review the board's images.

3 When you see a pin you want to delete, position your mouse ⬉ over the image until buttons appear at the top of the image.

4 Click **Edit**.

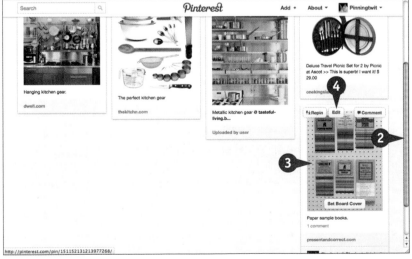

The Edit Pin window opens.

5 Click **Delete Pin**.

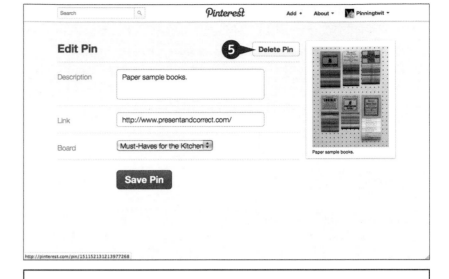

A confirmation screen pops up.

6 Click **Delete Pin**.

Pinterest deletes the pin and returns to the board. The pin has disappeared from the board.

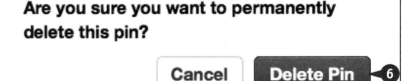

TIPS

Can I delete an image from my board, but somehow keep it just in case I decide I want it after all?
You may want to create a board such as Under Review or Second Thoughts, and place possible images there rather than deleting them entirely. Another possibility is to click **Like** on the pin and then delete it. That way you can find it on your Likes page.

Can I recover the pin if I change my mind?
You only get one chance to change your mind. When Pinterest asks, "Are you sure you want to permanently delete this pin?" you can click **Cancel**. However, if instead you click **Delete Pin**, the only way to recover the pin is to search for it.

Add or Edit a Board Description

You can give yourself and your followers a little extra information about your board by giving it a description. The description appears on the board's page as a subtitle to the board's title — and that is the only place the description appears. The description can be useful — for example, it can clearly define the board's focus — or it can serve whatever purpose you choose. Start on your profile page in the default boards view by clicking your name at the top of a Pinterest window. Once you have a board description, you can repeat the process to edit the description.

Add or Edit a Board Description

1 From your profile page, click **Edit** under the board to which you want to add or edit a board description.

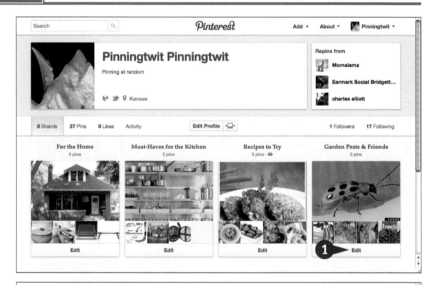

The Edit Board/*board name* window opens, where *board name* is the name of the board in question.

You can choose a new board title/name, type a description, or edit the category.

2 Type a description in the Description box.

3 Click **Save Settings**.

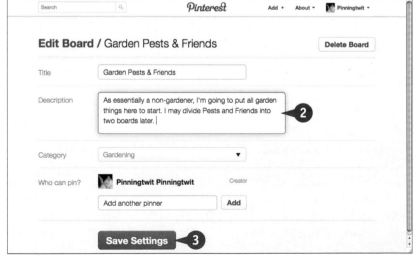

Pinterest returns to the board's page.

Ⓐ The description appears under the board's title.

4 Click the browser **Back** button (◀).

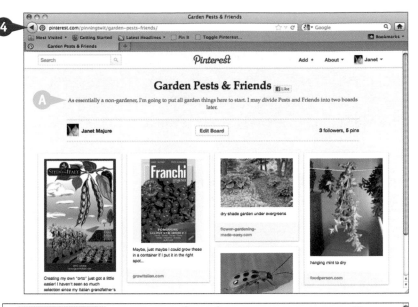

Pinterest returns to your profile page in the boards view.

Ⓑ The description is not available on the profile page.

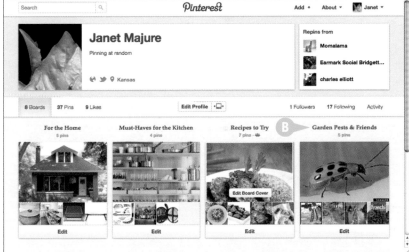

What should I include in my board description?

If you want your board to be ranked highly by search engines, be sure to include keywords in the description. For example, if you have a Wildflowers board, you might add a description such as *Annual and perennial wildflowers of Ohio woodlands*.

Can I change the board title when I add a description?

Yes. Simply click in the **Title** box, delete the current name, and type the new title. When you are done, remember to click **Save Settings**. Also, you can edit or change the board title at any time from the Edit Board page, whether or not you have or want a board description.

113

Add a Contributor to Your Board

Y ou can share your pinning efforts with a friend or relative when you add a contributor to your board. You may find that having contributors is a handy way to collaborate on a project, plan an event, or just to share a virtual scrapbook. Before you can add someone as a contributor, you must follow that pinner. It is best only to add contributors who you trust to participate in the way you intend. After they have accepted, the board carries a Group icon to signal that it is a group board.

Add a Contributor to Your Board

1 On your profile page, click **Edit** under a board you want to share.

The Edit Board/*board name* page opens, where *board name* is the name of the board where you are adding a contributor.

2 In the Who can pin? area, start typing the name of the contributor in the box.

Ⓐ Pinterest displays pinners you are following whose names match what you type.

3 Click the name of the pinner you want to add.

4 Click **Add**.

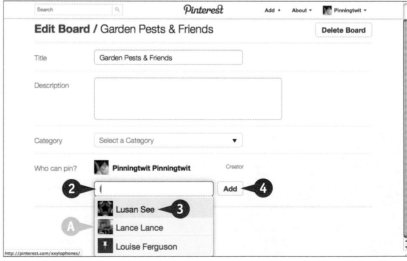

B The name of the contributor appears in the Who can pin? area.

C Pinterest confirms that it sent an invitation.

Note: You can add additional collaborators by repeating Steps **2** to **4**.

5 Click **Save Settings**.

Pinterest saves the changes on the board and returns to the board's page.

6 Click your name to return to your profile page.

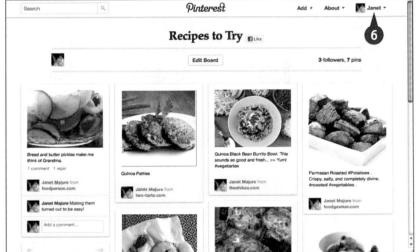

TIP

How will I know if the pinner has been added to my board as a contributor?

The pinner receives an e-mail notification and a notice on her profile page. She can click Accept to join the board or No Thanks to decline your invitation. You are then notified of her decision. After a pinner accepts an invitation to be a board contributor, the board appears on her profile page, and she appears on the board's page as a contributor. The board carries a Group icon (🔲) that indicates it is a group board. The contributor can remove herself at any time.

Remove Group Contributors

You can change your mind about who you have as contributors to a group board that you created. You might want to remove contributors because you have completed the project you were planning together. Maybe a contributor has ignored your requests to pin fewer images or to cease inviting other contributors. Whatever the reason, as the group creator, you can go to the Edit Board page to manage your group's members. You can tell at a glance who contributes and how they became contributors. You can remove those who you added, who other contributors added, or who have not responded to invitations.

Remove Group Contributors

As the Creator

1 Click your name.

Your profile page opens in the default boards view.

2 When you find the board you want to change, click **Edit**.

A The Group icon (🖼) indicates a group board.

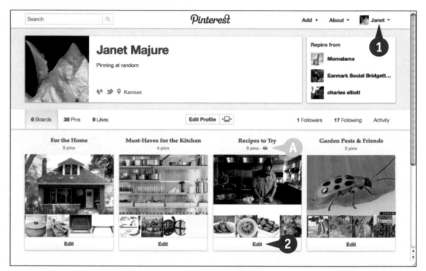

The Edit Board page opens for that board.

3 Scroll down until contributors appear.

B Pinterest identifies the creator.

C Pinterest shows who added each contributor.

D Pinners who have been invited but who have not responded appear faded and show the invitation.

4 Click **X** to remove a contributor.

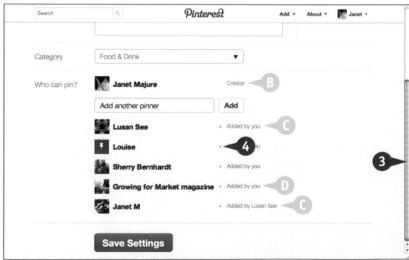

A confirmation window opens.

5 Click **Remove**.

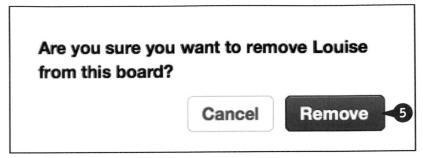

Pinterest returns to the Edit Board page.

The pinner you removed no longer appears in the list.

6 Click your name to return to your profile page.

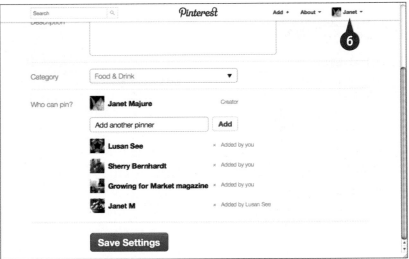

TIP

Does Pinterest have any tools that give me more control over the activities of contributors?

At this writing, Pinterest does not provide any tools to regulate contributors' board comments. As a result, you have two options when you create a group board. You can invite only people you trust and clearly communicate with contributors both your expectations and the consequences if the expectations are not met. Or, you can create the group board and adopt an attitude of *let us see what happens*. You can always remove contributors or the entire board if you are not pleased with the results.

Change Group Board as Contributor

You can remove yourself and those you added as contributors from a group board. You may want to leave because the board does not serve your purposes, or you find it is so active that it commandeers your feed. On the Edit Board page you can see other contributors and the board's creator, but as a contributor, you can only remove yourself and those people you added. Start by clicking your name at the top of a Pinterest screen to go to your profile page in its default, or boards, view.

Change Group Board as Contributor

1 Scroll down your boards page until you see the group board you want to change.

A The Group icon (🞖) helps you identify the board.

2 Click **Edit**.

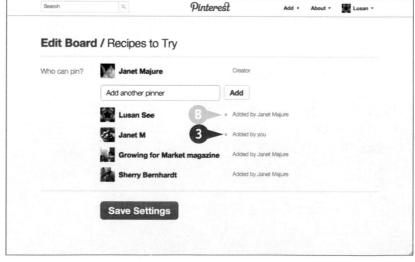

The Edit Board window opens.

B The contributors that you can change display an X next to their member information.

3 Click **X** next to the contributor you want to remove.

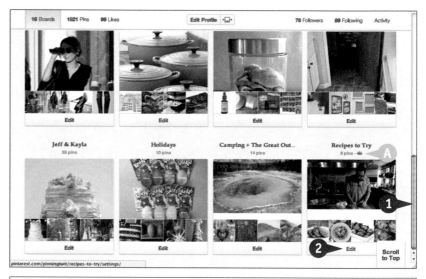

A confirmation window opens.

4 Click **Remove**.

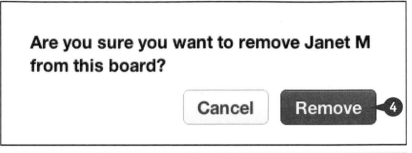

Pinterest returns to the Edit Board page.

The pinner you removed no longer appears in the list.

5 Click **X** next to your name.

A confirmation window opens.

6 Repeat Step **4**.

Pinterest removes you from the board and returns to your profile in the default boards view. The group board no longer appears there.

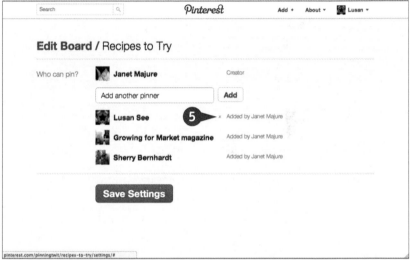

How does leaving a group board affect my ability to interact with the board?
You still can follow that board or the entire feed of the board's creator. You still can repin images from the board and add comments. You just cannot add images or contributors to the board. If you find that the board's images are not appearing in your feed, chances are that you never clicked Follow on the board's page. You need to do that now if you want it to be part of your feed.

Delete a Board

You can delete a board at any time in a few simple steps. Deleting underused boards can make pinning easier, because you will have fewer boards to choose from in the boards drop-down list. You can delete boards that you created to help you sort ideas for short-term projects. You also can delete group boards that have become overwhelmed with pins or pinners. Start by clicking your name at the top of a Pinterest screen to go to your profile page in its default, or boards, view. If you delete a board, though, remember you cannot recover it.

Delete a Board

1 Scroll until you see the board you want to delete.

2 Click **Edit** under the board.

The Edit Board window opens.

3 Click **Delete Board**.

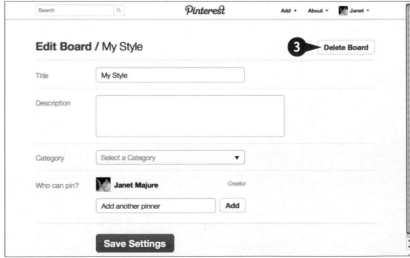

A confirmation window opens.

④ Click **Delete Board**.

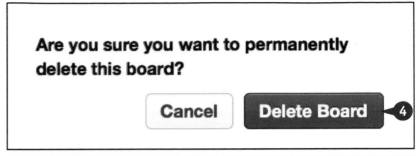

Pinterest deletes the board and returns to your profile page in its boards view.

⑤ Scroll through your boards to confirm the deletion.

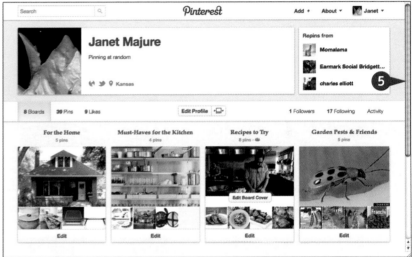

TIP

How can I keep some pins and still delete the board they are pinned to?
You must do this before you delete the board. Click the board's name or cover image on your profile page to open the board. Review all board images. When you find one you want to keep, position your mouse ▸ over the image until the Repin button appears. Click the button, and then click the board arrow. Select a board that you intend to keep, and then click **Pin It**. When you have done this with all pins you want to keep, then delete the board.

Delete a Comment Made on Your Board

As the curator of your boards, you can delete comments made on them by other people. Many reasons exist for why you may want to delete comments. Among them is that you may find a comment offensive or that you do not want redundant comments. Some pinners do not like to keep such unenlightening comments as *Aww* or *Love it!* or *:D*. Do remember that the commenter might similarly be offended if you delete a comment. Start at the Pinterest home page.

Delete a Comment Made on Your Board

1 Click the comment notice.

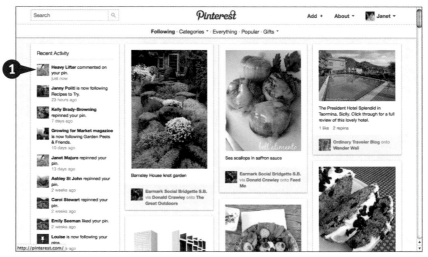

The pin's window opens.

2 Scroll down until you see the new comment.

③ Position your mouse ▶ near the X next to the comment.

A Remove Comment message box appears, and the X turns red.

④ Click the **X**.

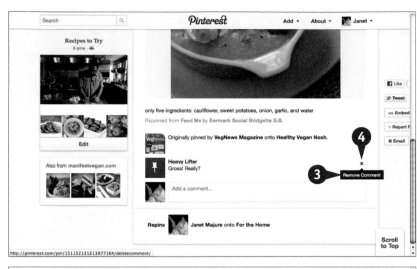

Ⓐ The comment disappears from the comments section.

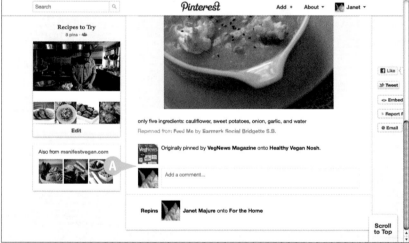

Is there any way I can recover a comment I accidentally deleted?

Unfortunately, no. Unlike with many similar actions, such as deleting a board, Pinterest does not ask you to confirm the deletion. When you click the **X** to remove a comment, it is gone.

How can I communicate directly with a commenter about comments?

If you click the commenter's name, Pinterest takes you to that person's profile page. You can leave a comment on a pin there, and the pinner will be alerted to your comment. You also can check to see if the pinner reveals a Twitter feed or personal website, as indicated by a gray Twitter bird icon or the gray Globe button (🌐), in the bio section of her profile. Those pages may provide contact information.

CHAPTER 6

Expanding Your Pinning Options

You can expand your pinning options by uploading images from your computer, by pinning from your mobile device, or by taking advantage of tools created by others.

Upload a Pin

You can create original pins when you upload images that you have on your computer. They could be photographs or other files in JPEG or PNG format. Uploading images directly to Pinterest is best when you have only an occasional image to upload. The maximum width Pinterest displays is 554 pixels. If you send a larger image, Pinterest will resize it. Your camera probably produces images two to three times that size. If you know how to reduce the size of your image to approximately 600 pixels wide, your uploads will go faster than trying to upload an image that is 2400 pixels wide.

Upload a Pin

1 Click the **Add+** button at the top of a Pinterest page.

The Add window opens.

2 Click **Upload a Pin**.

3 Click **Browse**.

The File Upload window opens.

4 Click the desired file.

5 Click **Open**.

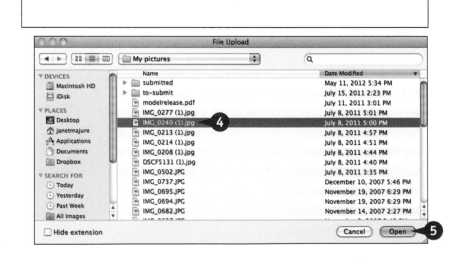

Pinterest uploads the image.

Note: Uploading may take a few seconds or longer, depending on the size of the image, the amount of site traffic, and the speed of your Internet connection.

6 Click the **Board** down arrow (▼) and select a board from the drop-down list.

7 Type a description.

8 Click **Pin It**.

Note: Do not click Pin It until the image appears in the upload window. Doing so may cause the upload to fail.

Pinterest opens the image in its pin window.

A The source reads Uploaded by user.

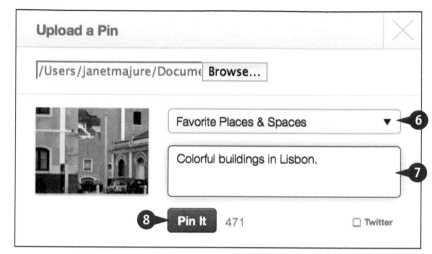

TIP

What is the best way to upload several images?
You are better off uploading your images to a site that specializes in storing images, such as Flickr.com or 500px.com, which has built-in Pinterest integration. Then, you can click a button at Flickr to share your image or images on Pinterest. Flickr has a handy upload tool that lets you upload and organize groups of photos, whereas Pinterest requires you to upload each image individually. Flickr, 500px, and similar sites also store information about the photo, such as its date and the camera used.

Edit a Pin's Source Link

You can edit a pin's source link after you have pinned or repinned the image. One good reason to do so is if you discover that the pin's link leads to the right website but not to the image and article where the image appears. This example uses a pin from a blog. It assumes you discovered that the pin's link went to the blog's main page, and that you searched the blog to find the article that included the image. Then, you copied the article's URL from the address bar in your browser. The steps begin at the image you want to edit.

Edit a Pin's Source Link

1 On the pin you want to edit, click **Edit**.

A Your browser reveals the pin's current link when you position your mouse ▶ over the image. In this case, the link goes to a general page on a website.

The Edit Pin window opens.

2 Type your link or press `Ctrl`+`V` to paste the link you copied into the Link box.

3 Click **Save Pin**.

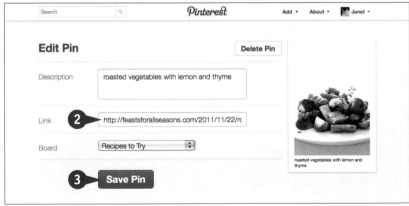

Pinterest returns to the pin page.

4 Position your mouse ꕔ over the image.

B The new link appears in your browser.

5 Click the image.

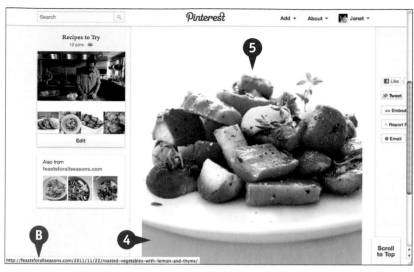

C The article where the pin is published appears in a new browser tab.

6 Click the pin's tab to return to the pin window.

TIPS

How do I find the article associated with the image?

The best way is to click through to the pin's website and use a search box on the site to find the content you need. If the site does not have a search box, go to **www.google.com**. In the search box, type a search term, then **site:**, and then the website's URL.

Can I use my Amazon affiliate code to link to a product that I pinned?

No, you cannot. Earlier, some people used such affiliate codes to get commissions on products when people went to Amazon and then purchased a product there. Pinterest began removing those codes, partly because spammers could edit links in this way.

Turn Screenshots into Pins

Y̶ou can turn screenshots into pins as a way to do such things as record the front page of your local newspaper's site on the day your baby was born. If you have your own site with numerous images on the front page that you would like to pin as a group, a screenshot works nicely for that, too. An online tool, at http://url2pin.it, makes easy work of it, although it works only for home pages. Start by copying the URL of the home page that you want to pin to Pinterest. A more complex site, http://pinstamatic.com, offers more options. This task uses url2pin.it.

Turn Screenshots into Pins

1 Go to **http://url2pin.it** in your browser.

2 Type or paste the URL of the screenshot you want.

3 Click **submit**.

After a moment, url2pin presents the screenshot.

4 Click the **Pin it** button.

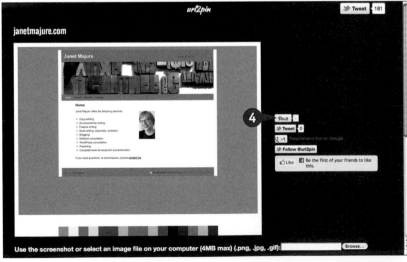

The Create Pin dialog box opens.

5 Click the **Board** ▾ and select a board on which to pin it.

Note: At this writing, the Create New Board option does not work through url2pin.it.

6 Edit the default description, if you want.

7 Click **Pin It**.

The window changes, and says Success!

8 Click **See your Pin**.

Pinterest opens to the new pin's window.

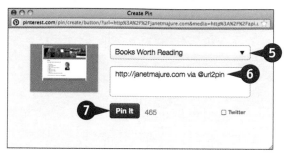

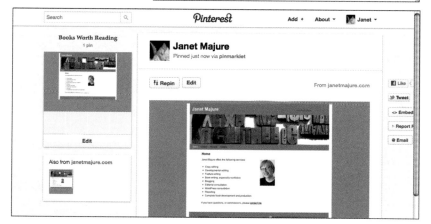

TIP

How do I pin more than the home page of a site?

First, go to the page you want capture. Then, take a screenshot using your computer's built-in tools or an add-on screen-capturing program. Next, upload the image to Pinterest just as you would any other uploaded image. On a Windows computer, press the `Print scrn` key. Then, click the **Start** button, click **All Programs**, click **Accessories**, and click **Paint**. When the Paint program starts, press `Ctrl`+`V` to paste the screenshot, and save it as a JPEG or PNG image. On a Mac, press `⌘`+`Shift`+`3`, and a screen shot will be saved to your desktop. Another option is to go to the website **http://pinstamatic.com**. Click the website icon, type the URL of the page you want, click **Preview**, and then pin it.

Create a Quote Image

If you want to post attractive quotes on Pinterest, you can use Share As Image to make the task easy. Share As Image, formerly known as Pin A Quote, lets you convert any text on a web page into an image that you can pin on Pinterest. The free version lets you create and post quotes, but you do not get to choose type style or color. The Pro version lets you choose among numerous type sizes, fonts, and color options for a modest price. For the free version, you install a bookmarklet, and you are ready to go.

Create a Quote Image

1 In your browser, go to **http://shareasimage.com/#free**.

2 Click and drag the bookmarklet to your browser's bookmarks bar.

Note: For more information on installing a bookmarklet, see Chapter 1.

The bookmarklet appears on the bookmarks bar.

3 Type a URL address that has a quote you like, for example, www.cs.virginia.edu/~robins/quotes.html.

4 Click and drag the mouse across the text you want to make into a quote image.

5 Click the **Share As Image** bookmarklet.

The Share As Image window opens.

A The quote appears.

6 Type the quote's author in the Source box.

Note: The font, size, and color options function only in the Pro version.

7 Click **Post**.

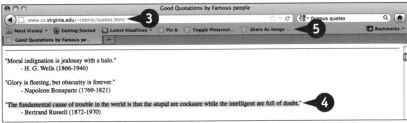

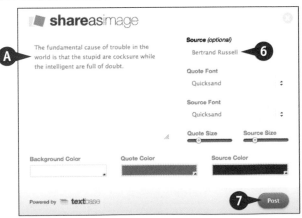

The quote image appears on the Share As Image website.

8 Click **Pin it**.

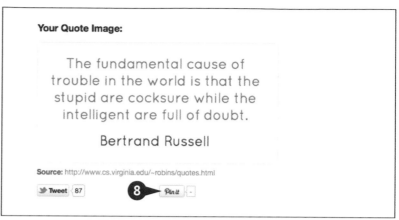

Your Quote Image:

The fundamental cause of trouble in the world is that the stupid are cocksure while the intelligent are full of doubt.

Bertrand Russell

Source: http://www.cs.virginia.edu/~robins/quotes.html

The Create Pin dialog box opens.

9 Click the **Board** ☑ and select a board from the drop-down list.

10 Click **Pin It**.

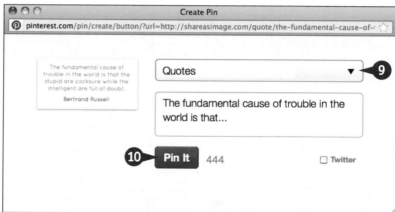

After a moment, the window changes and says Success!

11 Click **See your Pin**.

The pin's window opens on Pinterest.

Success!

Your pin was pinned to **Quotes**

See your Pin   Tweet your Pin   Share on Facebook

http://pinterest.com/pin/151152131214060649/

TIP

How will people know the source of the quote?
The Share As Image website is the source of the image, not of the quote. If you click the image to go to its source, your browser shows the quote image at www.shareasimage.com. The Share As Image website includes a link under the image to your source for the quote.

Make Stickies with Pinstamatic

Y ou can create informative board covers or alert followers to your plans with virtual sticky notes created through the free website Pinstamatic. The virtual sticky notes are images that look like the paper kind. Pinstamatic creates the sticky and then connects you to Pinterest to pin it. You can use such stickies to post quotes, to call attention to your plans — such as *Watch for my Hawaii pins!* — and even to point to websites that do not have images to pin. When you go to http://pinstamatic.com/new, you see an array of tools. This task focuses on stickies only.

Make Stickies with Pinstamatic

Make a Sticky Note

1 In your browser, go to **http://pinstamatic.com/new**.

2 Click the sticky note button.

The screen changes and shows Sticky.

3 Type the text you want on your sticky note.

A After a slight delay, the sticky note appears in a preview window.

4 Click **Pin**.

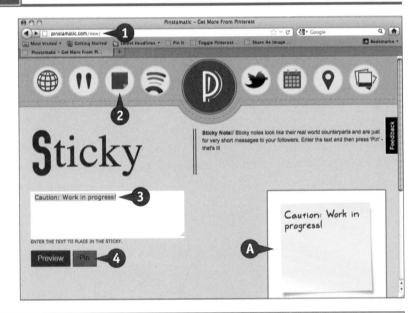

A Create Pin dialog box opens. It may take a moment for the image to appear.

5 Click the **Board** ▾ and select a board from the drop-down list.

6 Click **Pin It**.

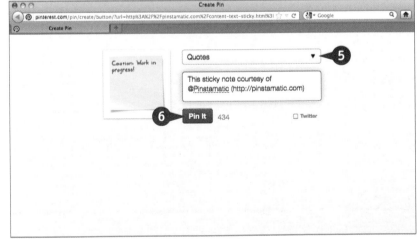

After a moment, the screen changes.

7 Click **See your Pin**.

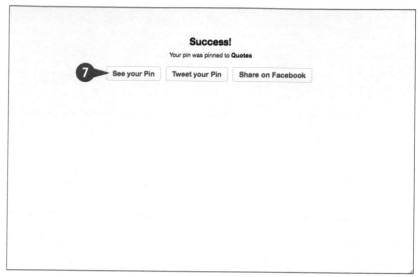

The pin's page appears.

TIPS

How do I use a sticky to link to a site without images?

You can mention the site in the text of your sticky note. Then, after you have pinned the sticky, hover your mouse ⬉ over the image on the pin's page. Click **Edit**. Then, in the Edit Pin window, type the site's URL in the link box.

How do I get help for a problem I had on Pinstamatic?

The site does not offer an online support knowledge base. However, you can send an e-mail support request to support@pinstamatic.com. Response times may vary.

Create a Map with Pinstamatic

You can create a great-looking and precise map with the Pinstamatic map tool. You can spotlight your business address, a favorite restaurant, or the hard-to-find location for a music festival. You simply type in an address or location name. It can be as general as *France* or as specific as a street address, and you can even make adjustments. Pinstamatic, in conjunction with Google, creates a map with an identifying note attached. Then, you follow the usual steps to pin the map to Pinterest. When Pinterest users click the pin, they are sent to a Google map of the spot.

Create a Map with Pinstamatic

1 In your browser, go to **http://pinstamatic.com/new**.

2 Click the map pin button.

The screen changes and shows Place.

3 Type the desired location in the Address box.

Pinstamatic offers possible locations as you type.

4 When the desired location appears in the list, click it.

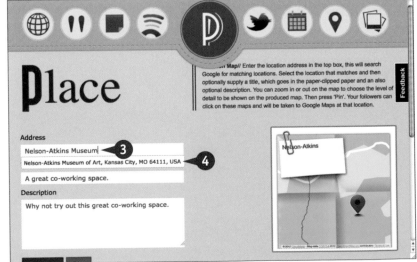

Pinstamatic creates a sample map.

5 Type a title.

A The title appears on the note under the paperclip.

6 Type a description.

7 Click **Pin**.

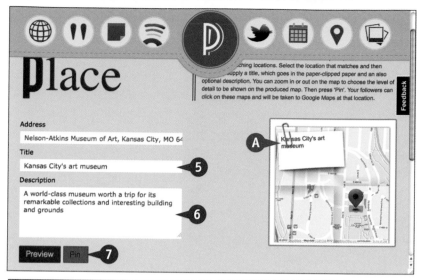

A Create Pin dialog box opens. It may take a moment for the image to appear.

8 Click the **Board** ▾ and select a board from the drop-down list.

B The description you typed at Pinstamatic appears.

9 Click **Pin It**.

Pinterest presents the usual series of screens when you pin an image.

TIP

How can I adjust the location?

Before you pin the map, scroll down below the boxes where you typed the location. A Google map points to the location with a map pin icon in the middle of the spot you typed in the address box. Click the **Pin** icon (A) on the Google map and drag it to the spot where you want it. The Pinstamatic map changes to match the pin's movement.

You can adjust the precise location by dragging the marker to the correct location and adjusting the zoom.

Pin Content with the Easypinner Browser Extension

The Easypinner browser extension gives you an even quicker way to pin new content at Pinterest. It goes one step further than the Pin It bookmarklet by letting you click in the window of the image you are viewing to start the pinning process. The Easypinner extension is available for the Chrome, Firefox, and Opera browsers. You need to open one of these browsers to install the extension. Once installed, Easypinner works on any site that allows you to pin its images.

Pin Content with the Easypinner Browser Extension

Note: This example uses Google Chrome.

1. In the Chrome browser, go to **https://chrome.google. com/webstore/search/ easypinner**.

2. Click **Add to Chrome.**

   The Easypinner dialog box opens.

3. Click **Add**.

A. Chrome adds the extension to your bookmarks bar and displays a message telling you so.

④ Go to a web page of interest.

⑤ Position the mouse ↖ over an image and click the Pinterest *P* symbol when it appears.

Ⓑ The *P* changes to a mini dialog box that shows the number of times the image has been pinned.

⑥ Click **Pin it**.

The Create Pin dialog box appears.

⑦ Click the **Board** ▾ and select a board from the drop-down list.

⑧ Add or edit the description.

⑨ Click **Pin It**.

Pinterest presents a series of screens after you pin an image.

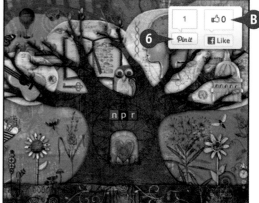

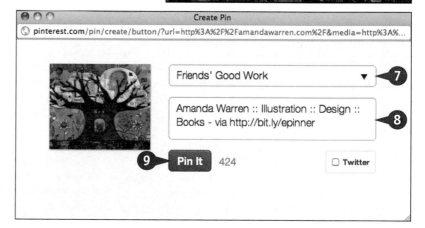

TIP

How do I add the Easypinner extension to Firefox?
In the Firefox browser, go to **https://addons.mozilla.org**, type **Easypinner** in the search box, and select **Easypinner for Pinterest** in the drop-down list that appears. The Easypinner for Pinterest add-on page opens. Click **+ Add to Firefox**. A confirmation window appears. Click **Install Now**, and Firefox installs the extension.

Add Pinning as a Right-Click Option

You can add pinning as a right-click function, thanks to the Pinterest Right-Click browser add-on. The Right-Click add-on lets you right-click directly on the image you want within the page where you see it. That saves a step compared with the Pin It bookmarklet. For people who routinely use the right-click function as they work on their computers, the Pinterest Right-Click add-on is a natural. It is available for the Firefox and Chrome browsers and even lets you pin background images.

Add Pinning as a Right-Click Option

Note: This example uses Firefox.

1 In the Firefox browser, go to **https://addons.mozilla.org**.

2 Type **Pinterest** in the search box.

3 Click **Pinterest Right-Click** in the list that appears.

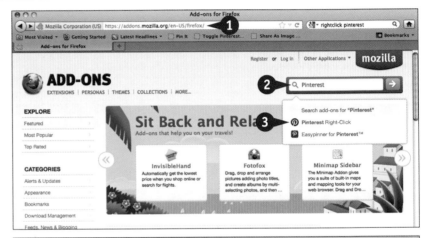

The Pinterest Right-Click add-on page opens.

4 Click **Add to Firefox**.

A A confirmation dialog box appears.

5 Click **Install Now**.

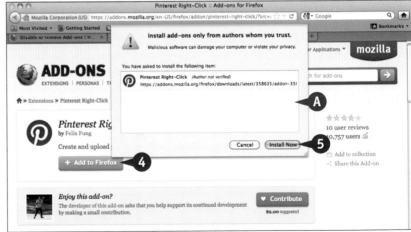

A dialog box opens.

6 Click **Restart Now**.

Firefox closes and restarts, returning to the Pinterest Right-Click page.

7 Go to a website of interest.

8 Right-click an image.

9 Select **Pin Image** in the drop-down list.

The Create Pin dialog box appears.

10 Click the **Board** ⊡ and select a board from the drop-down list.

11 Add a description.

12 Click **Pin It**.

Pinterest presents a series of screens after you pin an image.

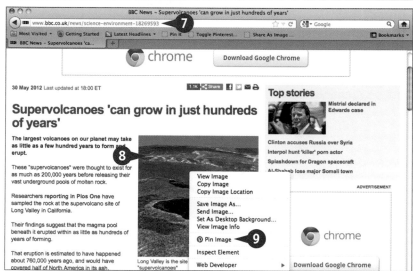

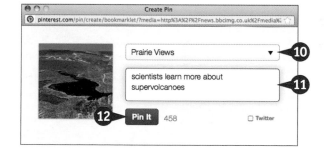

TIP

How do Pinterest Right-Click and Easypinner compare?

Easypinner users see a red *P* in the corner of an image when they move their mouse ▸ over it. A single click on the *P* produces a Create Pin dialog box with a description drawn from the source.

Pinterest Right-Click requires two clicks — a right-click to open a context menu and then a click on Pin Image — to arrive at the Create Pin window that lacks a description. However, Pinterest Right-Click allows you to click a background image and click Pin Background Image from the context menu, whereas Easypinner does not.

Add a Video to Your Board

You can add dynamic content to your boards by adding videos. That way, you can pin computer tutorials, craft-making demonstrations, or favorite music or news videos. Click the Videos link at the top of the Pinterest home page to see videos other people are pinning. A symbol on each video pin even tells the source of most videos. Click a video to go to its pin page, and you can watch the video without leaving Pinterest. The pinning process is as easy as pinning a still image, but it has a Play button in the middle of it.

Add a Video to Your Board

1 Starting on the host video web page, click the **Pin It** bookmarklet.

The screen changes to show images and videos available for pinning.

2 Position your mouse ▶ over the video image.

The Pin It button appears.

3 Click **Pin it**.

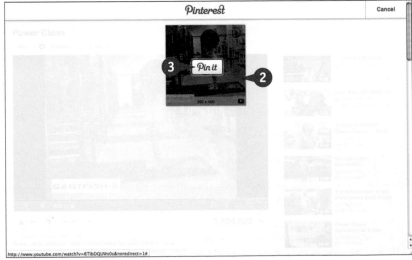

The Create Pin dialog box opens.

④ Click the **Board** ⬝ and select a board from the drop-down list.

⑤ Type a description.

⑥ Click **Pin It**.

The dialog box changes to Success!

⑦ Click **See your Pin**.

Ⓐ The pin window opens in a new tab.

⑧ Click **Play** (▶) to view the video.

Ⓑ You can click the tab to return to the original video page.

TIPS

How does a video pin differ from an image pin?
Viewers can add comments or repin videos. Videos just look different in feeds, because they display a Play button (▶) in the middle.

How can I change the part of the video that displays in the feed?
Unless you created the video, you cannot. The image in the feed is a slice from the middle of the video.

Use the Pinterest App on Your iPhone or iPad

You can use your iOS device and a fully integrated Pinterest app to view, repin, and comment on Pinterest images. Although multiple apps related to Pinterest are available, the app from Pinterest Inc. is the official app. With it, you can log in to Pinterest and do just about anything you might do on Pinterest through your computer's browser. The first step is to download and install the app, simply called Pinterest, from the Apple App Store. Navigation is only slightly different from the browser version. You will be updating your Pinterest in no time.

Use the Pinterest App on Your iPhone or iPad

1 Tap the **Pinterest** icon.

The Pinterest app launches.

2 Tap **Login**.

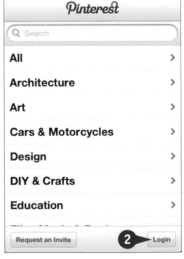

The Pinterest login screen appears.

③ Tap your preferred login method.

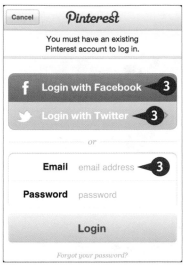

A dialog box about push notifications appears.

Note: This dialog box appears only the first time you start the Pinterest app from your smart phone.

④ Tap **Don't Allow**.

Note: If you prefer, you can click OK to allow push notifications.

TIPS

If I do not already have a Pinterest account, can I sign up for one through the Pinterest app?
Yes. To sign up for an account using a Pinterest app, click **Join Pinterest** when you launch the app, and then complete the sign-up process. You can use your Facebook or Twitter account, or sign up using your e-mail address.

Can I use the Pinterest app without logging in to Pinterest?
Yes. The first screen you see lets you search or view pins by category. Just tap the category you want to view and scroll through the image. Unless you log in, you are not able to pin, like, or comment on pins.

continued ▶

Once you have installed the Pinterest app and you are logged in to your Pinterest account, the easiest way to pin is through repinning. If you want to create a fresh pin, the Pinterest app leads you through the creation process with the camera on your iPhone or iPad. You also have access to your profile page and some account settings. If you want to create a new pin from a website on your iOS device, use the Pin It bookmarklet through Safari, just as you would on your desktop browser.

Use the Pinterest App on Your iPhone or iPad (continued)

The Pinterest app opens to the most recent pin among those you are following.

5 Slide your finger across the screen to scroll down through the feed.

6 Tap **Explore**.

The category feeds list appears, with All being the equivalent of the Everything link in the browser version.

7 Tap the category you want to view.

The feed for that category appears.

8 Tap an image that interests you.

The image opens.

9 Tap **Repin**.

Note: You may need to scroll down to see the Repin button.

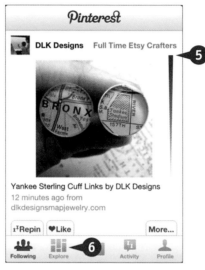

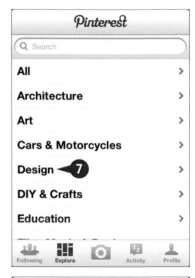

The Repin screen appears.

10 Tap **Board**.

The Choose a Board screen appears.

11 Tap a board.

The Repin screen reappears.

12 Tap **Repin**.

The app repins the pin, and a confirmation message appears.

13 Tab **Back** to return to the feed.

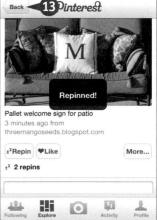

TIP

What are the options on the bottom of the pin screen?

The pin screen options are

 Ⓐ Like: Marks image as one you like

 Ⓑ Comment: Opens keyboard to create comment

 Ⓒ Following: Shows feed of those you follow

 Ⓓ Camera: Launches camera to create pin

 Ⓔ Activity: Shows your activity

 Ⓕ Profile: Opens your profile

 Ⓖ More: Opens menu with sharing, saving, and other options

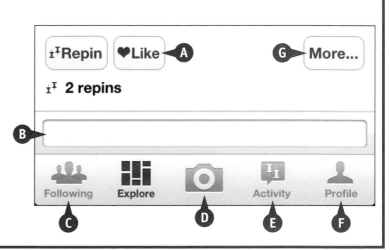

Access Pinterest from Other Mobile Devices

N o matter what kind of mobile device you use — including Android, Windows, and iOS devices — you can access Pinterest. You simply start your device's browser and go to the mobile version of Pinterest, at http://m.pinterest.com. Although the mobile version does not allow you to create new pins or boards, you can like, repin, and comment on existing pins. You also can search and view standard feeds as well as your pins, likes, followers, and more. Pinterest recently released an Android app available at Google Play. Other third-party apps are available, but they may not be reliable.

Access Pinterest from Other Mobile Devices

1 In your mobile browser, go to **http://m.pinterest.com**.

2 Click **Login**.

The login screen appears.

3 Type your Pinterest e-mail address.

4 Type your Pinterest password.

5 Click **Login**.

A You also can use your Facebook or Twitter logins.

Pinterest opens to the feed of pinners you follow.

6 Click the **magnifying glass** (🔍).

A drop-down list opens with options that are equivalent to links at the top of an ordinary Pinterest page.

7 Click **Everything** in the drop-down list.

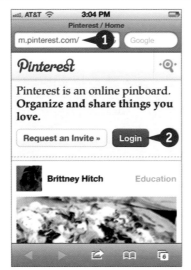

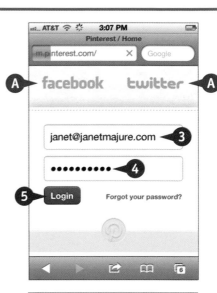

8 Click **All.**

The All feed appears.

9 Click your profile image.

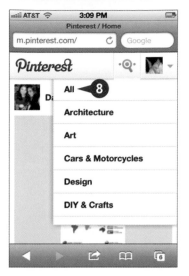

10 Click **Profile.**

The mobile view of your profile page opens.

B You can link to mobile views of your pins, likes, followers, and boards or pinners who you are following.

You can also link to your boards.

TIPS

How can I search in the mobile application?
Click the **magnifying glass** (🔍). Click in the search box. Using your mobile device's keyboard, type your search term and then click **Go** or your equivalent of **Enter** on your mobile device. The mobile Pinterest page opens a search page using your search term.

Can I install the Pin It bookmarklet on my mobile browser?
If you are using an iOS device, you can install the bookmarklet on Firefox or Safari on your desktop or laptop computer. Then, when you synchronize your iPhone or iPad with your computer using iTunes, the bookmarklet will be added to the Firefox or Safari browser on your device. At this writing, no bookmarklet exists for other mobile devices.

CHAPTER 7

Promoting Your Business or Blog

You can be among the savvy business people and bloggers who are building their brands through Pinterest by being helpful, not by direct selling.

Determine If Pinterest Is a Good Fit

With a little creativity, your business or blog can take advantage of the soaring popularity of Pinterest. It offers possibilities for boosting your brand presence, selling products, and leading people to your website. Pinterest has proven to drive more sales than Facebook. Before you launch a Pinterest campaign or presence, however, it is worthwhile to consider whether Pinterest is a good fit for your business. If it is not, you still can use and benefit from the medium, but it may require more effort than you want to spend.

Some Categories Fit Naturally

Seven of the top ten most popular categories of pins on Pinterest lend themselves readily to a Pinterest campaign. Those seven are food and drink, do-it-yourself and crafts, home decor, women's apparel, wedding and events, hair and beauty, and kids. If your business or blog addresses any of those interests, you probably should consider including Pinterest in your social media campaign strategy. Look at the statistics available at www.repinly.com/stats.aspx to see if your business activity is a natural fit with current Pinterest users.

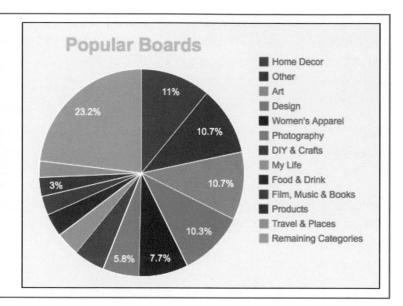

Some Categories Require More Effort

Some businesses and blogs are less-obvious Pinterest candidates. They include businesses or blogs that cater to other businesses or those that focus on lower-income consumers. Research indicates that Pinterest users have above-average income and are more likely to be female than male. If you have a service business, say car and homeowner's insurance, you still can use Pinterest to promote your business, but it will not be by putting up beautiful product pictures. You instead may pin good images related to your insurance business, such as an infographic on which car models are more likely to be stolen.

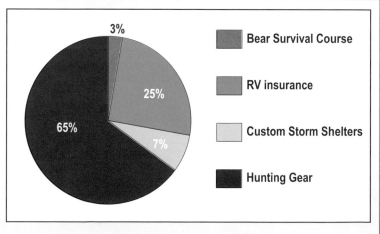

Comfort with a Public Presence

Because Pinterest is entirely public, you cannot choose who sees and who does not see your pins or Pinterest profile. You cannot control who likes or who repins your images. You can edit or delete comments made on your pins on your boards — but not on repins. As a business owner, you also do not have control over how anyone responds to your print or electronic advertising, but being on a social medium may make you feel more exposed. If you are not comfortable with that kind of exposure, Pinterest may not be right for you.

Make Pinterest Part of a Plan

As tempting as it may be to jump on board, you are well served if you consider Pinterest part of a broader social-media presence for your company or blog. Decide in advance what you want from your Pinterest presence. You may aim to push more traffic to your home page or to drive direct purchases. Keep in mind, however, that Pinterest does not allow advertising or overt promotions. You can use your Pinterest activity to keep information and images flowing to your Twitter followers and Facebook friends. Another option is to build your brand by being a useful resource. Whatever your goal, you will be more likely to reach it with a plan.

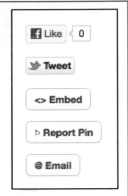

Consider the Time Factor

If you read much about Pinterest users, you frequently see remarks about the service being *addictive*. That is good for you if it means users are spending more time looking at content, including yours. It is bad if it means you or your staff is spending hours looking for and pinning images when

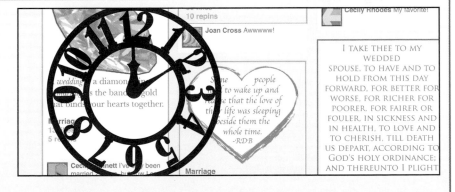

you really need to attend to other business needs. To pin successfully, you need to pin regularly. Determine how much time you have to spend before committing to Pinterest. If you cannot make a commitment, it may be better not to start, as your followers may not like being abandoned.

Add a Pin It Button to Your Site

One of the best ways to get others to pin images from your site is to include a Pin It button next to images you hope to have pinned. Pinterest provides the code needed to make this happen. You need to be able to edit your web pages to add the Pin It button code. If you do not know how, your webmaster should be able to take care of the matter with ease. Details of the editing process vary according to the program you use for website management.

Add a Pin It Button to Your Site

1 In your browser, go to **http://pinterest.com/about/goodies**.

2 Scroll down to the Pin It Button for Web Sites section.

3 Type the URL of the page.

4 Type the URL of the image.

5 Type a description of the image.

6 Scroll down until you see the code boxes.

7 Click and press `Ctrl`+`C` to copy the code in the first box.

8 Open the page where you want to add the button in your website management software.

This example uses WordPress in a new tab of the browser.

Note: If you use a program such as Dreamweaver, start the program on your desktop.

9 Click where you want the button to appear on your page, and then press `Ctrl`+`V` to paste the code.

10 Click **Update** to save the changes.

Note: If you are using another page-editing program, use its usual method of saving.

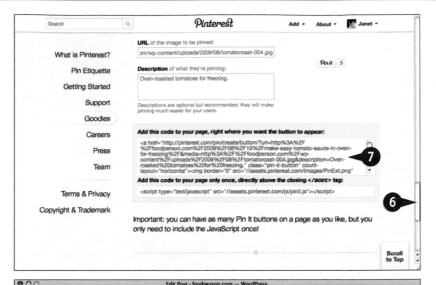

TIP

What does the Pin Count menu refer to in the box beside the spot where I enter the URL?
It lets you choose whether to include a number beside the Pin It button and, if so, in what format. The number corresponds to the number of times that image has been pinned at Pinterest. You can click the double arrow (⊞) next to Pin Count and try out the options. A sample of how the Pin It button would look appears below the Pin Count menu.

continued ▶

nce you have a Pin It button next to an image on your website, site viewers need only to click
the button to pin the image. If they are not currently logged in to Pinterest, however, Pinterest
will prompt them to log in before they can complete the pin. Details of adding the Pin It button
may vary somewhat depending on the website-management software you use. This example uses
WordPress.

Add a Pin It Button to Your Site (continued)

11 In your browser, click the **Pinterest/Goodies** tab.

12 Click and then press `Ctrl`+`C` to copy the code in the second box.

13 Open the file where you want to add the code in your website-management software.

This example opens the footer.php file in WordPress in a new tab of the browser.

Note: If you use a different site-management program, open footer.php or the equivalent in your program.

14 Click just before the closing `</body>` tag, and press `Ctrl`+`V` to paste the code.

15 Click **Update File** to save the changes.

Note: If using another page-editing program, use its usual method of saving.

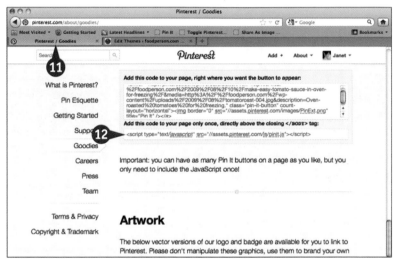

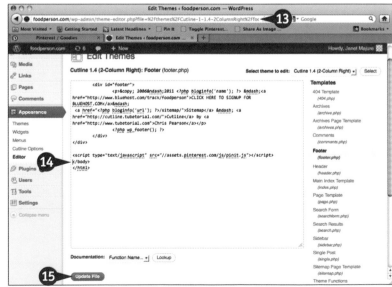

A WordPress confirms the update.

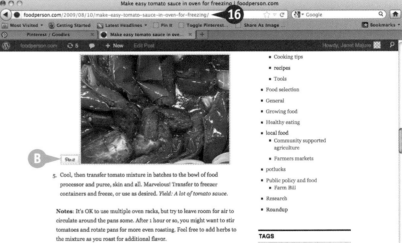

16 In your browser, type the URL to the page where you inserted the button.

B The Pin it button appears where you placed the first bit of code.

Why did this process not work for me, when I followed the directions exactly?
It may be a matter of how your website is set up. If you have another JavaScript script operating on your site, for example, it and the Pinterest code may interfere with each other. Try deleting the second bit of code you added to your site. Save the changes, and then check the page to see if the Pin it button appears. If that does not work, check with a website consultant.

Add a Follow Button to Your Site

Y ou can encourage visitors to your website to become your followers on Pinterest. Pinterest offers four follow buttons. While you are logged in at Pinterest, you choose the one that you want, copy the code that appears, and paste the code in the desired spot on your website. After that, a website visitor who clicks the button automatically is routed to your profile page at Pinterest, where the visitor can click the Follow All button to follow you, click Follow under any individual board, or click on boards to see all you have pinned to them.

Add a Follow Button to Your Site

1 In your browser, go to **http://pinterest.com/ about/goodies**.

2 Scroll down to the "Follow Button" for Websites section.

3 Click the follow button you like.

Code appears, already highlighted for copying.

4 Press Ctrl+C to copy the code.

5 Open the file in which you want to place the button code in your website-management software.

This example uses WordPress in a new tab of the browser.

6 Click where you want the code and press Ctrl+V to paste the code.

7 Click **Update File** to save the changes.

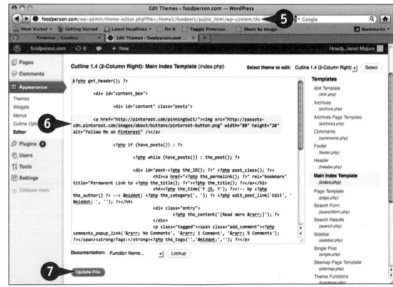

8 In your browser, go to your website.

Ⓐ The Pinterest button you chose appears in the spot you placed it. This example says merely *Pinterest*. See other appearance options in Step **3**.

9 Click the **Pinterest** button.

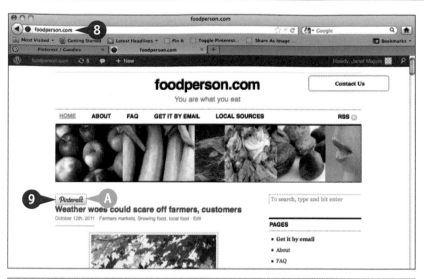

Pinterest opens to your profile page.

Ⓑ You, as the creator, see an Edit Profile button. Other viewers will see a Follow All button.

TIPS

What is the best place to put the Follow button on my website?

The answer depends in part on your website design, but, generally the header is a good spot, as is the footer, the About page, a sidebar, or in a template for every individual article.

Can I do more to encourage people to follow me through the button?

Yes. You can add text next to where the button appears, saying something like, *Click the button to see my Pinterest page, and then click Follow All to see my pins in your feed*. You also can add encouraging text of that nature in your profile description.

Add a Product to the Gifts Section

Pinning a product to the Gifts feed at Pinterest is a simple process, but you can make the process more valuable when you combine your biggest image of the product and the best URL for possible purchases. Chances are good that your website does not automatically display the biggest image of your product, which improves your page's loading time. You need to find the best image on your site or upload a big image. Then, you edit the image's link so that it goes to the exact product page.

Add a Product to the Gifts Section

1 In the pin window of the item you want to add to the gift section, click **Edit**.

Note: The pin should be a large version of the product image.

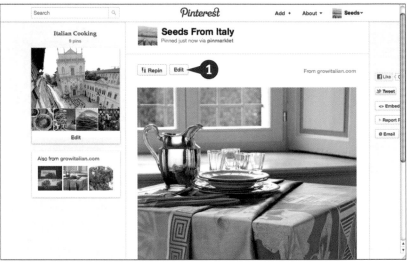

The Edit Pin window opens.

2 Type the price, using the dollar sign or British pound sign.

Ⓐ The price appears across the corner of the image.

3 Type the product page URL in the Link box.

4 Click **Save Pin**.

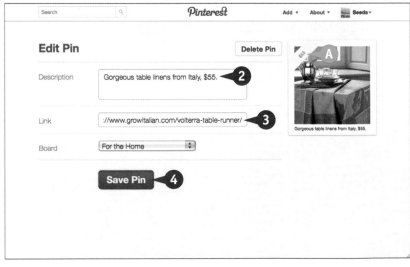

The pin page opens.

5 Click the image.

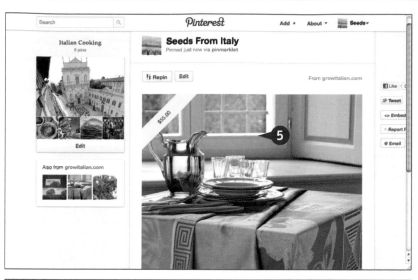

B Your browser opens the product page in a new tab.

Should I pin the product to a gifts board or to some other board?

Try pinning it to a topical category, such as For the Home, so that people looking at home decor images see it. By including a price, the image automatically appears in the Pinterest Gifts feed. In addition, you can repin it to your gifts board. Repinning makes it appear twice in the feed of someone following all your boards. You must decide if that is a good or bad thing.

Should I make all product pins gift pins?

No. Doing so dilutes the power of your gift pin. When you use the gift option sparingly, followers see that your items with prices are particularly well suited as gifts, and are not just other products you are promoting.

Pin Images and Link to Your Website

When your business is not particularly visual, you still can take advantage of Pinterest by pinning images related to your business and then editing the links to go to your website. You can pin quotes, images that you have uploaded to Pinterest, or graphics that are relevant to your business. When you edit the pin, the source that appears on the pin window is the link that you put in the Edit Pin window. Be sure you also link to the original source of the image if it is not your work.

Pin Images and Link to Your Website

1 In the pin window of the image to which you want to link, click **Edit**.

A The source appears above image.

The Edit Pin window opens.

2 Make sure the description includes the image source's complete URL, including http://.

3 Type your URL in the Link box.

4 Click **Save Pin**.

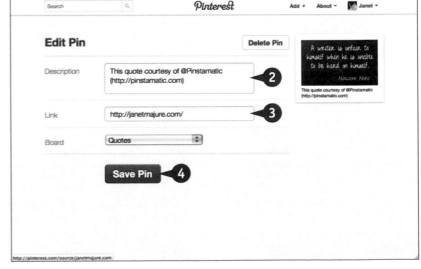

The pin window reappears.

B The source appears as your website.

C The original source appears as link under the image.

5 Click the image.

The image opens to your website.

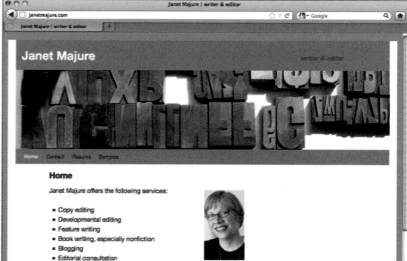

What kind of image should I use to link to my business page?

Good choices include a screen capture image of your home page, assuming it has a good visual impact. Other ideas include professional images — photos or computer graphic images — of subjects related to your business. They could be pictures of hands for your massage business or favorite stamps for your stamp shop. As long as an image is eye catching and you have rights to it, it is a good choice. You can search for public domain images at http://commons.wikimedia.org. Also, try www.flickr.com, especially images that are part of its Commons collection and U.S. Government collections.

Add a Guest Board

You can engage your customers and attract new ones when you add a guest board to your Pinterest page. To do it, think of a topic that your customers, potential customers, or colleagues might like to contribute to. Then, create a board on that topic and invite potential contributors to contact you. When they do, you can start following their boards, which allows you to add them as contributors. Once they accept your invitation to contribute, they can pin to your guest board, and the guest board appears on their Pinterest page.

Add a Guest Board

1 Click **Add+** at the top of a Pinterest pages.

The Add dialog box appears.

2 Click **Create a Board.**

The Create a Board dialog box appears.

3 Type a board name.

4 Click the **Board Category** down arrow (🔽) and select a category from the drop-down list.

5 Click **Create Board**.

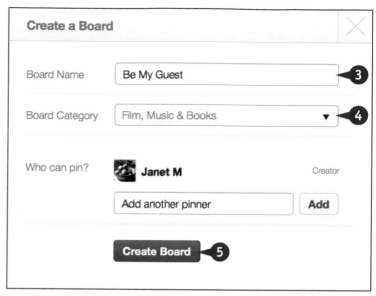

The new, empty board appears.

6 Click **Edit Board**.

TIP

Where can I see examples of guest boards?

You can find some by using Pinterest search. Simply type **guest board** in the search box at the top of a Pinterest page and press **Enter**. Search results based on pins labeled **guest board** appear. Click the **Boards** link at the top of the search results. Scroll through the boards to see some guest boards—and expect to see some other *guest* topics, such as guest rooms. Or, try http://pinterest.com/namabakery/guest-board as an example.

continued ▶

Having a guest board can be a fun process for everyone and expands your presence, as your guests' followers will see the guest board pins in their feed, too. Incorporate the guest board as part of your overall marketing plan by notifying customers by e-mail, on your website, and via other social media. Let them know of the board, and tell them what they need to do to contribute. If you want, encourage them to invite their friends to contribute, too.

Add a Guest Board (continued)

The Edit Board screen appears.

7 Type a description.

Note: Include information about how to become a guest pinner for the board.

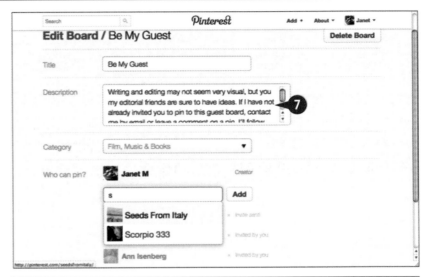

8 Start to type the name of someone you are following.

Note: Pinterest shows possibilities as you type.

9 Select the name you want from the drop-down list.

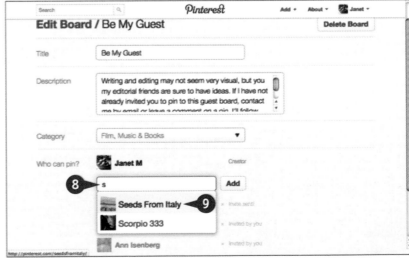

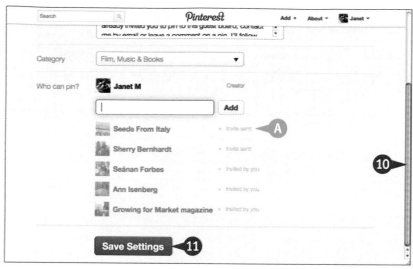

Ⓐ The invitee appears under the Add box.

⑩ Scroll to the bottom of the screen.

⑪ Click **Save Settings**.

The board page opens.

Ⓑ A description appears under the board title.

Note: You may now start pinning to the board. Those you invited can start pinning as soon as they accept your invitation.

TIPS

Should I include my e-mail address in the description so that people can contact me?

If you are comfortable posting your e-mail address publicly and tolerant of receiving junk e-mail, you can include your e-mail address. You can also set up an e-mail address specifically for the board to keep your requests separate from your spam and regular e-mails.

Why is the name of a person who is following me not showing up as a possible contributor in the Add box?

You have to follow a pinner to add him or her as a possible contributor. Click the **Followers** link on your profile page to find the person, and then click **Follow** next to his or her name.

Conduct a Contest

Conducting a contest is a fun way to generate interest for your business. One easy method is to ask people to pin images of a particular kind — such as a photo of their messy room for your home-organizing business. Ask contestants to include a hashtag of your choice, such as *#mycontest,* when they pin the image. For more information on hashtags, see Chapter 4. You can repin the entries to your Pinterest contest board. Set a contest time frame, prize, and winning criteria, and then announce the contest to your e-mail list and post it on other social media. Post the rules on your website.

Conduct a Contest

1 On your profile page in the boards view, click **Edit** under the board you intend to use for your contest.

The Edit Board screen appears.

2 Type a description.

Note: Include key rules and the URL to your website where you post details.

3 Click **Save Settings**.

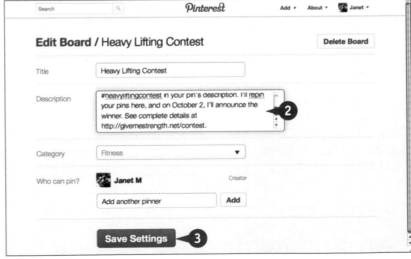

A The board page appears with your description. The URL is not a live link, but users can copy it and find the page.

4 Type your hashtag term in the search box and press Enter.

Images with the hashtag appear.

5 Position your mouse ▸ over an image and click **Repin**.

The Repin window opens.

6 Click the **Board** down arrow ▾ and select a board from the drop-down list.

7 Click **Pin It**.

Pinterest pins the repin to your contest board and, after a pause, returns to the search results.

8 Repeat Steps **5** to **7** for all new contest entries.

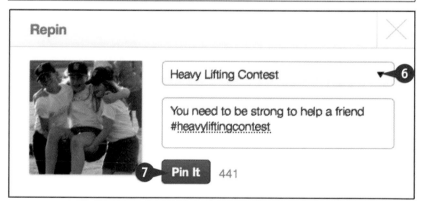

TIPS

Are there other ways to run a contest?
Yes, there are. You can find examples by typing **contest** into the Pinterest search box. The first search results show pins with the word *contest* associated with them. Click the **Boards** link on the search results page to see contest boards.

What if I have a contest and no one enters?
If that happens, you did not promote the contest well. Be sure to take advantage of your e-mail lists, your website, and other social media, such as Facebook and Twitter, to let likely contestants know and to update them with deadline reminders or the number of entries. You can also enlist a few friends to enter. Remember, all their followers will see their contest pins. Having an appealing prize helps too.

Add Text to an Image

You can encourage people to click on an image by adding text to the image. One picture may be worth a thousand words, but you can get a thousand and ten words by adding text. Make sure the text is informative, not hard sell. The idea is to pin an image that encourages repinning and eventually clicking to your Pinterest profile and then to your website where the image is based. Start by selecting a high-quality image with an area where text would display nicely and edit it at www.picmonkey.com, a simple online picture-editing site. You can do the same thing with most any graphics program.

Add Text to an Image

1 In your browser, go to **www.picmonkey.com**.

2 Click **Edit a photo**.

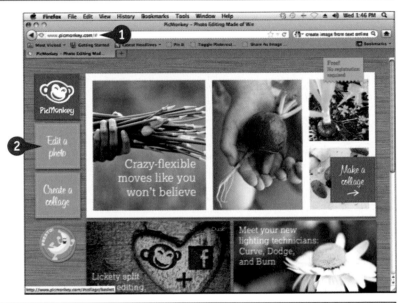

A file upload window opens.

3 Click the image you want to upload.

4 Click **Open**.

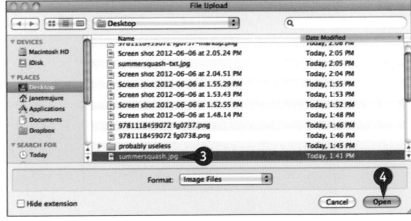

The image opens in the PicMonkey editor.

5 Click **P**.

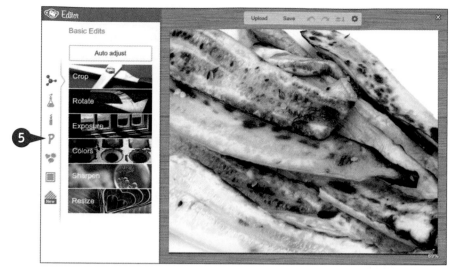

The sidebar changes to display text options.

6 Click a typeface.

7 Type your message in the box.

Note: At this writing, PicMonkey does not wrap text, so you need to press Enter where you want to insert line breaks.

8 Click **Add**.

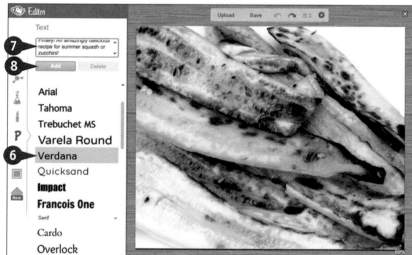

TIP

How do all the PicMonkey text-editing tools work?
PicMonkey offers many ways to alter the text you add to your image. The best way to learn them is just to try them out. You can try the options by going to **www.picmonkey.com** and clicking one of the sample images there. When it opens, click **P** to open the text editor. Follow Steps **7** and **8** of this task, and then experiment with the text tools.

continued ▶

When you add text to an image, you can add key bits of information that you think are of interest to prospective customers. You may have the same information in the image description, but by including the words within your eye-catching image, you increase the odds that Pinterest viewers will click the image to learn more. You also increase odds that someone may repin the image. Repins, of course, increase your pin's exposure across Pinterest.

Add Text to an Image (continued)

Your text and the Text tools box appear on top of your image.

9 Use the tools in the Text tools box to adjust size, color, and other text details.

10 Click and drag the text box to position it where you want it.

Note: The text tools box moves out of the way during this operation.

11 When you are satisfied, click **Save**.

A dialog box opens.

12 Click **Save photo**.

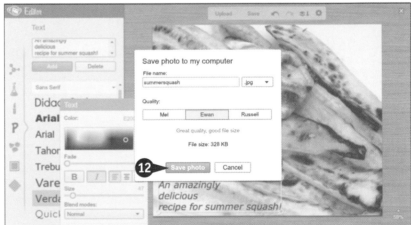

A dialog box opens.

13 Type a name in the Save As box.

Note: Default name is original filename.

14 Click the **Where** double arrow (⬍) to locate the folder where you want to save the edited image.

15 Click **Save**.

The edited image is saved to your computer at the location you specified, and PicMonkey invites you to upload another.

16 Click **Cancel**.

You can now go to http://Pinterest.com and upload your text-enhanced image.

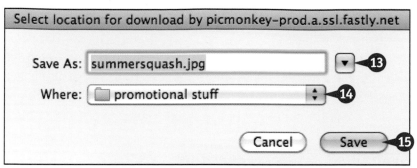

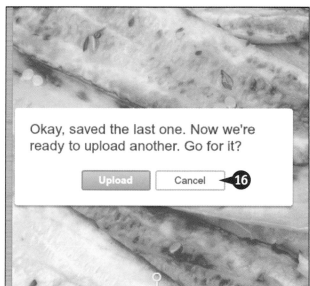

TIP

Can I pin the text-enhanced image to Pinterest but keep the image plain on my website?
Yes. Leave the plain image on your site. Then, simply pin the enhanced image by uploading it. Edit the pin to add the URL of the image location on your site. When people click the pin, Pinterest should send them to the URL you specify.

View Pins from Your Website

You can see at a glance all images pinned from your website by combining your domain name, such as *example.com,* with the Pinterest source URL. The page shows all the original pins from your site, comments made on the pins, number of repins, and number of likes. You also can see and click the name of the pinner and the pinboard to which the image is pinned. Or, you can click the image to open its pin window. This quick, visual overview can give you clues as to what content to pin and ideas for content to add to your website.

View Pins from Your Website

1 In your browser, go to **http://pinterest.com/ source/yourdomain.com,** where *yourdomain.com* represents your website's domain.

The page displays all pins from *yourdomain.com.* This example uses foodperson.com.

2 Scroll down to review all the pins.

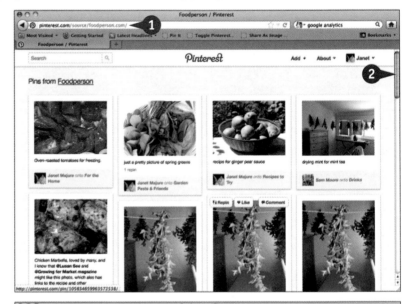

A For each pin, note the number of likes and repins.

Note: Some images repeat.

3 Click an image that has several repins.

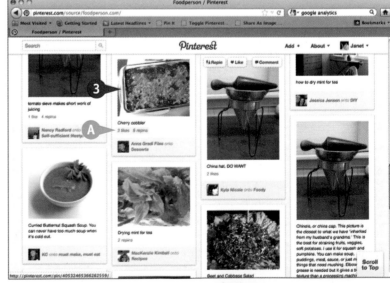

The pin's page opens.

4 Scroll down to see repin information.

B You can view the pinboard names onto which the image has been repinned for ideas on why pinners chose that image.

In this case, the pin and repins appear to go to recipe or dessert boards.

5 Click the browser **Back** button ( ).

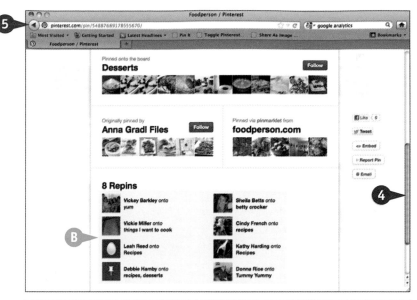

The source page reappears.

6 Repeat Steps **2** to **5** for other popular pins.

TIPS

Why does the same image show up multiple times on the source page?

Each appearance of the image represents one instance of a person pinning from your website, either by using the Pin It bookmarklet or by entering the URL using the Add + link on the Pinterest home page. Those original pins are distinct from repins of images seen on Pinterest.

Is it better to have pins or repins?

They are both good because anyone following a person who pins or repins your image sees the pin in their default Pinterest feed. If the pinner or repinner has many followers, the pin will get many views. Those viewers may not repin the image, but they may click it and arrive at your website.

Analyze Your Pinterest Activity

Y ou can get an idea of how far your Pinterest activities are taking you thanks to a couple of free websites, Pinpuff and PinReach. They give scores based generally on the number of pins, repins, followers, and so on. More useful is the fact they show you the information in one convenient place. PinReach requires registration but provides graphs, pictures of the most popular pins, and a list of influential followers. Pinpuff is simpler, both to use and in terms of information offered, and provides a summary of activity. However, it lets you look at other pinners' Pinterest influence too.

Analyze Your Pinterest Activity

1 In your browser, go to **http://pinpuff.com**.

2 Type an e-mail address.

Note: It does not have to be the address you use at Pinterest.

3 Type your Pinterest username.

4 Click **Calculate Your Pinfluence**.

A After a moment, the page changes and shows your score. The average score is 32.

5 Click **here**.

Your score profile page opens in a new tab.

B Your reach and activity scores appear with suggestions on how to improve them.

C Your most popular boards appear.

D A summary of pinning activity involving your Pinterest account appears. On future visits, the statistics will show changes since your previous visit.

6 Scroll down.

Board information appears.

E Followers, pins, repins, and likes for each board up to 20 appear.

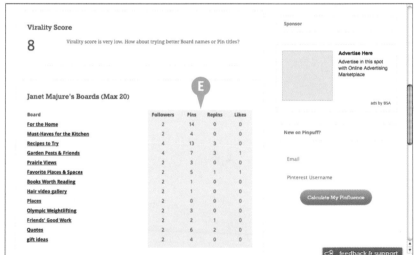

CHAPTER 8

Expanding Your Audience

Once you are feeling at home at Pinterest, you can start thinking seriously about expanding your audience. You can do it by sharing your pins outside of Pinterest and by following others to let them know you exist. The likely result is you gain followers, an affirmation that you are choosing well when you pin images.

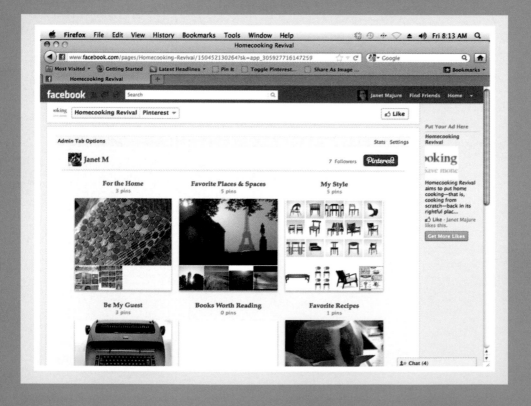

Share Your Pins on Facebook

The fastest way to increase the audience for your pins is to share them on Facebook, especially if you share them with Everyone, not just Friends. If you signed up with Pinterest using your Facebook account, you may already be linked to Facebook and perhaps only need to adjust a setting. At this writing, Pinterest only links to personal Facebook accounts, not business pages. A few clicks on your Edit Profile page let you make the connection and start pinning, indirectly, to Facebook.

Share Your Pins on Facebook

1 Click your name and select **Settings** from the pop-up menu.

The Edit Profile page opens.

2 Scroll down until you see the Facebook On-Off toggle.

3 Click the **Link to Facebook Off** button to toggle to On.

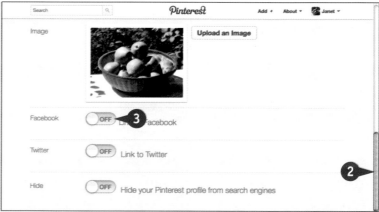

A Facebook Pinterest app window pops up.

4 Click **Go to App**.

After a moment, the app window disappears.

Ⓐ The Add Pinterest to Facebook Timeline toggle appears.

Ⓑ A link to Find Facebook Friends on Pinterest appears.

5 Click the **Add Pinterest to Facebook Timeline Off** button to toggle to On.

The Pinterest app window reappears.

6 Click **Add to Facebook**.

After a moment, the app window disappears.

7 Click **Save Profile**.

Your Pinterest pins now appear automatically on your Facebook Timeline.

TIPS

My Edit Profile page shows me as linked to Facebook and has Add Pinterest to Facebook Timeline turned on, but my pins do not appear on Facebook. What should I do?
First, go to the **Edit Profile** page, and click the **On** toggle to turn off the link to Facebook. Click **Save Settings**. Then, click the link to turn Facebook back on, click **Add Pinterest to Facebook Timeline** back on, and click **Save Settings**.

Are there other steps I can take if my pins still do not appear on Facebook?
Yes. While logged into Facebook, go to **www.facebook.com/settings?tab=applications** and click **Apps** in the left sidebar. Click **Edit** next to Pinterest, and then click the drop-down list in the Posts on your behalf section. Make sure Everyone, Friends, or some other group is selected.

Link to Twitter

When you link to Twitter, you can share your pins with your Twitter followers. If you signed up with Pinterest using your Twitter account, you may already be linked. If not, linking your Twitter and Pinterest accounts is a simple process that starts on your Edit Profile page at Pinterest. Once your accounts are linked, you will be able to post your Pinterest pins to Twitter, although such posts are not automatic.

Link to Twitter

1 Click your name and select **Settings** from the drop-down list.

The Edit Profile page opens.

2 Scroll down until you see the Twitter On-Off toggle.

3 Click the **Link to Twitter Off** button to toggle to On.

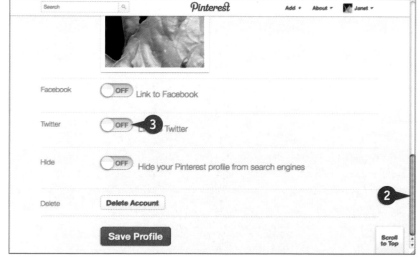

A Twitter authorization window opens.

④ Type your Twitter username or e-mail address.

⑤ Type your Twitter password.

⑥ Click **Sign In**.

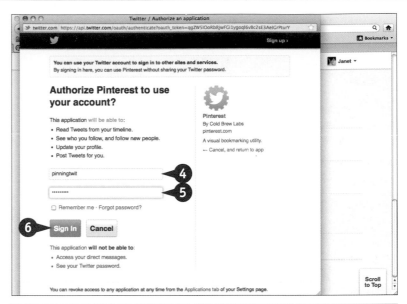

The Twitter window disappears.

⑦ Click **Save Profile**.

Pinterest saves your settings and returns to your profile page.

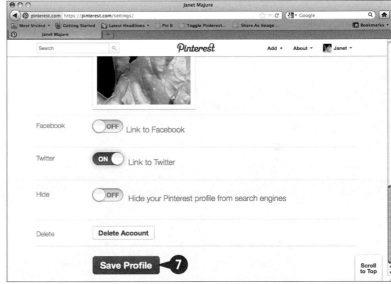

TIPS

If I signed up with Pinterest using my Facebook account, can I connect with Twitter also?
Yes. You are free to spread your Pinterest pins across both of these social networks. It can be handy to do so, as you may have different audiences for your different social networks.

If I connect to Twitter, will my past pins show up in my Twitter feed?
No. If you want them to appear, you need to open each pin, click the **Edit** button, and click the **Tweet** button. A Twitter window then appears where you can click a second **Tweet** button to put the pin on your Twitter feed.

Share Pins Through Twitter

When your Pinterest account links to Twitter, you have at least two ways to post to Twitter, or *tweet,* images that you like on Pinterest. You can post to Twitter as you repin or pin images, or you can post images when you view them without pinning them to your boards. You can tweet images on a pin-by-pin basis rather than potentially overwhelming your Twitter feed with every pin you make. Your tweet includes a URL that followers can click, which takes them to the pin page at Pinterest.

Share Your Pins Through Twitter

1 Click **Repin** on an image.

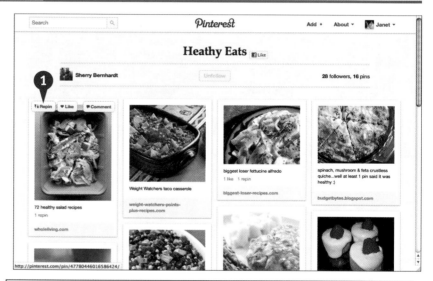

The Repin dialog box opens.

2 Click the **Board** down arrow (▾) and select a board from the drop-down list.

3 Type a description.

Note: The description on the pin appears by default.

4 Click the **Twitter** check box (☐ changes to ☑).

5 Click **Pin It**.

Your pin goes to your Twitter feed, and a confirmation box appears. After a second or two, the box disappears.

The Pinterest page where you began your repin returns.

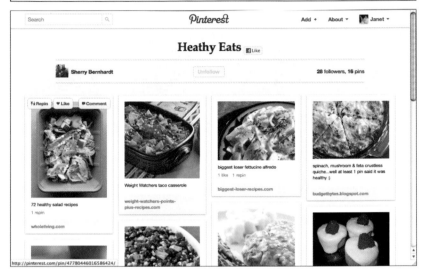

TIP

How can I share a pin without pinning or repinning?
To share a pin without pinning or repinning, follow these steps:

1 On a pin page, click **Tweet** to open the Share a link on Twitter dialog box.

2 Edit the text, but do not change the URL.

3 Click **Tweet**.

Your pin goes to your Twitter feed, and the dialog box disappears. A confirmation flashes on the screen before the pin page reemerges.

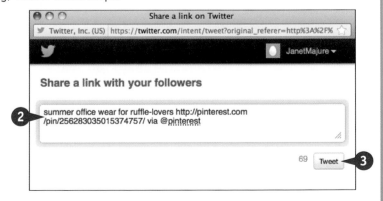

185

Add a Pinterest Tab to Your Facebook Page

You can expand the audience for your Pinterest boards by sharing them on your business Facebook page. It is as simple as installing an app. The Pinterest Page App lets you show all your Pinterest boards or a selected board at Facebook, and your Facebook page visitors can click the boards within Facebook to see your individual pins. It lets visitors to your Facebook page like pins or send them to their friends.

Add a Pinterest Tab to Your Facebook Page

① In your browser, go to **www.facebook.com/add.php?api_key=305927716147259&pages**.

② Click **Add Pinterest Page App**.

Note: This example assumes you are logged into Facebook.

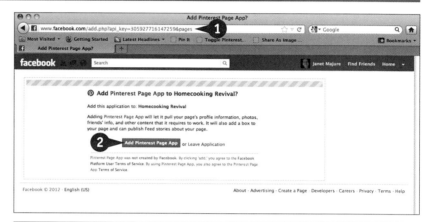

Your Facebook page opens.

③ Click the **Pinterest** button.

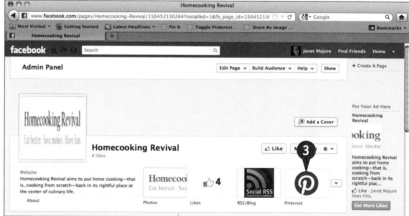

The Tab Settings screen opens.

4 Click **Authorize the Tab Application**.

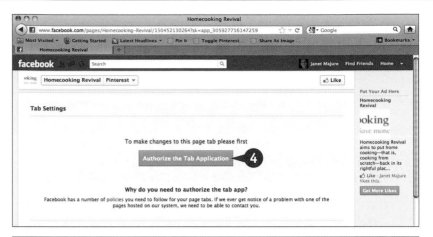

The Pinterest Page App window opens.

5 Click **Go to App**.

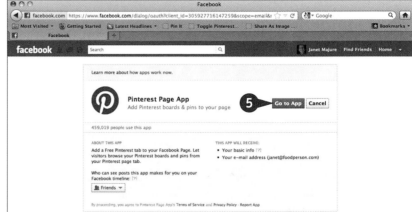

TIP

If someone likes a pin when she sees it on my Facebook page, does that register as a like on my Pinterest page?
It does not. Facebook *likes* and Pinterest *likes* are two different statistics. If a pin gets *likes* on Facebook, however, Pinterest shows the number of Facebook *likes* next to the Facebook thumbs-up on the image's pin page.

continued ▶

The Pinterest Tab app includes a button that takes your business Facebook page visitors straight to your Pinterest page. The app also offers a link where you can see statistics about visitors to the Pinterest tab. This app is handy for business pinners at Pinterest, because your Pinterest account cannot link directly to your business's Facebook page. Instead, the basic Pinterest connection is to your personal Facebook page.

Add a Pinterest Tab to Your Facebook Page (continued)

The Pinterest Tab Settings screen appears.

6 Type your Pinterest username.

7 Click the **Share Options** check box (☐ changes to ☑).

8 Click **Save Settings**.

Facebook saves the settings.

9 Click **View Tab**.

Your Pinterest boards appear on your Facebook page.

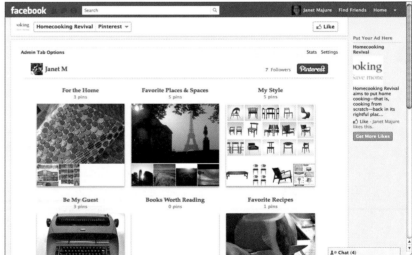

TIP

How do I select one board for display on my Facebook page?
On the Pinterest Tab Settings screen, click the **Show Pins from Selected Pin Board** option (◯ changes to ◉). A box appears where you type the URL for that board. You can find that URL by opening the board at Pinterest and copying from your browser's address box.

Add a Pinterest Link to Your E-mail

Including a Pinterest link on all your e-mail messages lets your e-mail correspondents know that you are on Pinterest. It also makes it easy for them to find you there. All you need to do is to include a *signature*, or automatically included closing, on your e-mail messages. The precise steps for creating a signature vary from one program to another, but they all let you create a signature, save it, and apply it to your e-mail messages automatically.

Add a Pinterest Link to Your E-mail

1 Click the **Settings** button (⚙▾).

2 Click **Settings** on the pop-up menu.

Note: This example uses Gmail.

3 Scroll down to the Signature area.

4 Type a signature message, such as Follow me on Pinterest!

5 Select the word or words that you want to link.

6 Click the **Link** button (⊡).

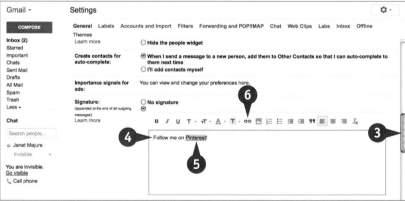

The Edit Link dialog box opens.

7 Type the URL for your Pinterest profile page.

Note: Your Pinterest profile page is http://pinterest.com/username.

8 Click **OK**.

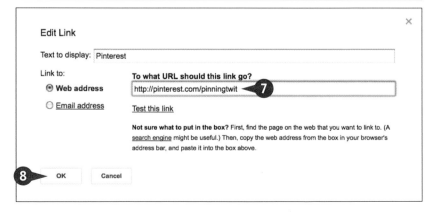

Ⓐ The settings page shows your link in the Signature box.

❾ Scroll to the bottom of the page.

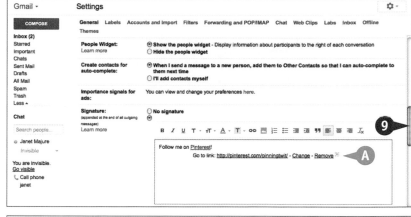

❿ Click **Save Changes**.

Gmail saves your signature and returns to the main Gmail page.

TIP

Can I link to a board rather than my profile page?

Yes. Each board has its own URL. In general, the URL is http://pinterest.com/*username*/*boardname*/, where *username* is your Pinterest username, and *boardname* is the name of your board, all lowercase and with hyphens instead of spaces between words. To be sure, though, go to your Pinterest profile page, click the board to open it, and copy the URL that appears in your browser's address bar.

Embed Pins on Your Blog or Site

You can encourage visitors to your website or blog to visit your Pinterest page by embedding pins on your website. You need to know a little about how your website works to complete this task. Specifically, you need to know how to make changes on your site, and it is best to know how big an area, as measured in pixels, you have available for your embedded pin. Once it is embedded, the pin provides four links: to the pin, to the source of the pin, to your Pinterest profile, and to the Pinterest home page.

Embed Pins on Your Blog or Site

1 On a pin page, click **<> Embed.**

The Embed Pin on Your Blog dialog box opens.

2 Type the desired image width.

Note: The width can be the same or smaller than what the dialog box displays.

A Pinterest automatically adjusts the height to maintain the pin's proportions.

3 Click in the box, which selects the code, and press **Ctrl**+**C** to copy.

④ Open your website editor.

Note: This example uses a widget in WordPress.

⑤ Type a headline for your embedded pin.

⑥ Press `Ctrl`+`V` to paste the code in the desired location.

⑦ Press `Ctrl`+`S` to save your changes.

⑧ Click your website name to view it.

Note: Step **8** will vary depending on your site editor.

The embedded pin appears where you placed it.

Ⓑ The image links to the pin.

Ⓒ Link to the source.

Ⓓ Link to your Pinterest profile.

Ⓔ Link to the Pinterest home page.

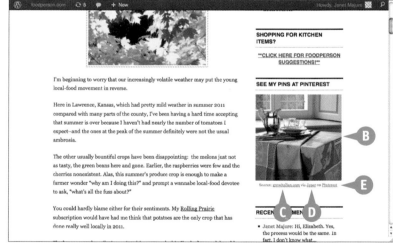

Add a Pinterest Plugin on WordPress

Y ou can make your Pinterest connection with your WordPress website or blog easier with a plugin. As you might expect, many options are available, including several social-sharing plugins that include Pinterest buttons along with buttons for sharing on Facebook, Twitter, and other social networks. If you want your viewers to think *Pinterest!* when they see your site, though, a dedicated Pinterest pinning plugin such as Pinterest "Pin It" Button is ideal. Plugins are for self-hosted WordPress sites. If you have a blog at WordPress.com, you can include Pinterest via the Sharing options at WordPress.com.

Add a Pinterest Plugin on WordPress

1 In your WordPress dashboard, position your mouse ▶ over Plugins, and click **Add New** in the flyout menu.

The Install Plugins panel appears.

2 Type **pin it button** in the search box.

3 Click **Search Plugins**.

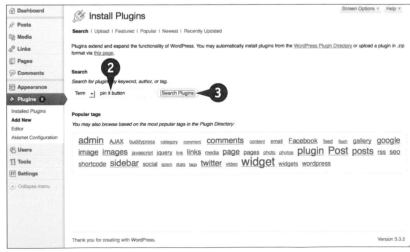

The search results appear.

④ In the Pinterest "Pin It" Button area, click **Install Now**.

A confirmation dialog box appears.

⑤ Click **OK**.

The screen changes, and WordPress installs the plugin.

⑥ Click **Activate Plugin**.

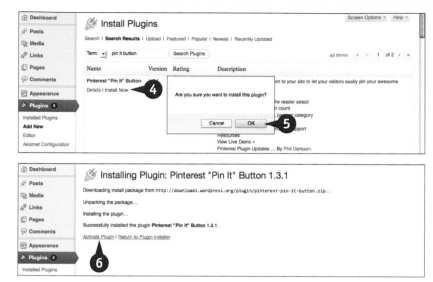

WordPress activates the plugin, and opens the Plugins module.

Ⓐ Pin It Button appears in the left menu bar, which lets you view button settings.

TIPS

How does the Pin It Button plugin behave compared with the Pin It bookmarklet?

The Pin It Button plugin and Pin It bookmarklet operate exactly the same way when the plugin is using its default settings. That is, when someone clicks the Pin It button on your website, a selection of possible images to pin appears, just as if the person had clicked the Pin It bookmarklet. The advantage of the plugin is that it gives readers a reminder with every post.

What settings are available with the Pin It Button?

You can specify that the Pin It Button is associated with a specific image, rather than letting the user choose from all options on a page. It also lets you decide on which pages to publish the button and whether it appears above or below content. It even lets you customize the button and show pin counts.

Promote Your Pinterest RSS Feeds

You have RSS feeds based on your Pinterest activity, and you can use them to promote your pins there, even to people who are not Pinterest members. RSS, which stands for *really simple syndication*, allows people to subscribe and view your activity in their *feed readers*. Feed readers let users view, all in one place, a feed or list of all activity from URLs they have subscribed to. You have feeds for your overall Pinterest account and for your individual boards. You can identify and copy your feed URLs and then send e-mail messages to contacts to ask them to subscribe.

Promote Your Pinterest RSS Feeds

1 Click your name on a Pinterest page to go to your profile page.

2 In your browser's address box, type **feed.rss** after the URL and press **Enter**.

Your Pinterest RSS feed appears.

3 Scroll down to see what your feed looks like.

4 Click in the address bar and press **Ctrl**+**C** to copy the URL.

5 After opening your e-mail program, click **Compose** to create a new message.

6 Type an address in the To box.

7 Type a subject.

8 Type a message and press **⌘**+**V** to paste the URL of your feed.

9 Click **Send**.

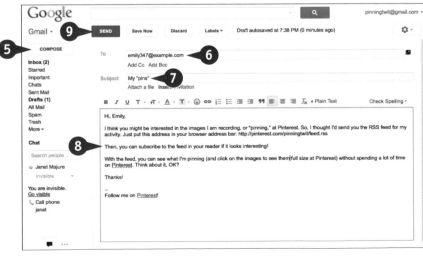

10 In your browser, type **http://pinterest.com/** *username/* where *username* is your Pinterest username.

Your Pinterest profile page opens.

11 Click a board title for which you would like an RSS feed.

A The board opens.

12 Type **feed.rss** in the address bar at the end of the board URL, and press `Enter`.

The board RSS feed appears.

13 Repeat Steps **3** to **12** for as many boards as you want.

Can I create feeds from anyone's Pinterest activity?

Yes. You can go to any member's profile page or board, type **feed.rss** at the end of the URL for the profile or feed, and press `Enter`. When the feed appears, you can subscribe to the feed you want in the feed reader of your choice.

What do I do if I do not have a feed reader?

Many feed readers are available for free. Popular web-based feed readers include Google Reader and Feedly, which also has versions for iOS and Android. Other readers download feeds to your computer or mobile devices. They include FeedDemon for Windows and RSSOwl for Windows, Macintosh. and other operating systems. Numerous other readers exist, though, including ones for your iOS and Android devices.

Use Repins to Find Pinners

*O*nce you have been active on Pinterest for a while, you can identify pinners you may want to follow by paying attention to pinners whose images you have repinned as well as the pinners who have repinned images from your boards. The activity view of your profile page leads you to those from whom you have repinned, and the Pinterest home page points to those who have repinned your images. Take a look at both sets of pinners, and follow those whose boards appeal to you.

Use Repins to Find Pinners

1 Go to **http://pinterest.com/** *username*/**activity** in your browser, where *username* is your Pinterest username.

2 Scroll through the activity page until you see an image you repinned.

3 Click the name of the pinner you repinned.

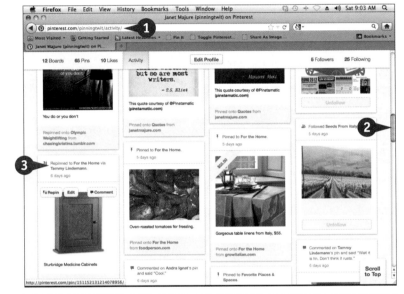

The pinner's profile page opens.

4 Scroll through the boards to determine your interest.

5 Click **Follow All**.

Note: If you prefer, you can click **Follow** under individual boards.

The Follow All button changes to Unfollow All.

6 Click your browser's **Back** button (◀) and repeat Steps **2** to **5** to select additional followers.

7 Click **Pinterest**.

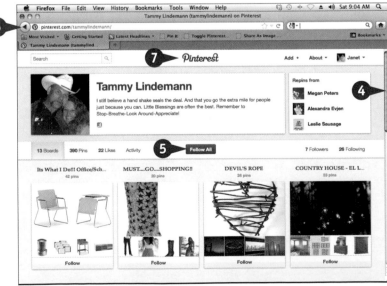

The Pinterest home page opens.

⑧ Click the first item saying that someone repinned your pin.

The pin page opens.

⑨ Scroll down to see the repin information.

⑩ Click the name of the pinner who repinned the image.

The pinner's profile page opens.

⑪ Scroll through the boards to determine your interest.

⑫ Click **Follow All**.

Note: If you prefer, you can click **Follow** under individual boards.

The Follow All button changes to Unfollow All.

⑬ Click **Pinterest** to return to the home page, and repeat Steps **8** to **12** to follow more pinners who repinned your pins.

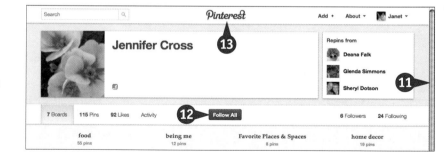

TIPS

How can I tell if someone who has repinned an image is someone I am already following?

You go to the pinner's profile page. Once there, the Follow/Unfollow button above the pinner's boards will read *Unfollow All* if you already are following that pinner. If you are following one of the pinner's particular boards, the link under that board will read *Unfollow*.

How does following others expand my audience?

People notice when others follow them. Thus, when you follow someone, chances increase that the person in turn takes a look at your profile and your boards. If he or she sees something of interest, chances are that pinner will start following you.

CHAPTER 9

Putting Your Pinterests to Work

Once you get the hang of Pinterest, you can use it to plan events, build a gift registry, save great ideas for use in the classroom, post your resume, and promote your favorite cause.

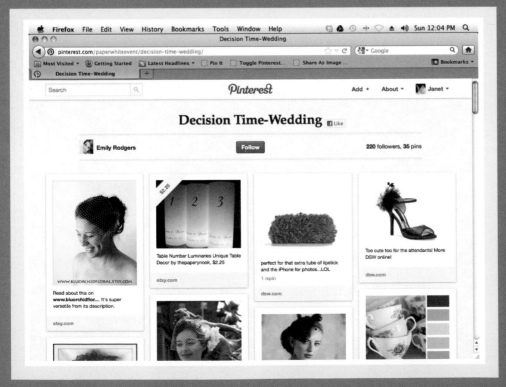

Access Resources for Teaching

You can put your imagination to work by using Pinterest for teaching. Teachers are using Pinterest to organize holiday ideas, to pin current events, to engage students, and to share with and get ideas from other teachers. The best way to get started is to find and review other teachers' boards. Once you begin following some teachers' boards, you are sure to see ideas that you want to repin. When you do, you can click the pin to see the source, and the source likely has even more classroom ideas for you.

Access Resources for Teaching

1 Position your mouse ▸ over Categories and select **Education** from the drop-down list.

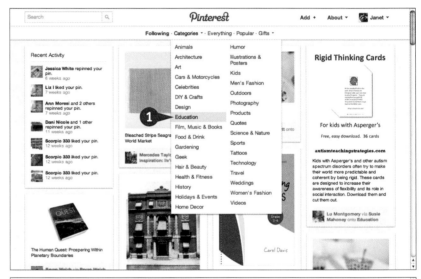

The Education category feed appears.

2 Scroll down to sample the pins available and the boards to which they are pinned.

3 Click a board that looks interesting.

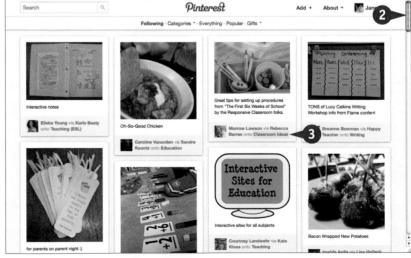

The board opens.

4 Scroll down to see what is pinned.

5 Click the pinner's name.

The pinner's profile page appears.

6 Scroll down to see the possibilities.

7 Click **Follow** under any board you want to follow.

A Follow changes to Unfollow.

8 Click your browser's **Back** button (◀) until you return to the Education feed.

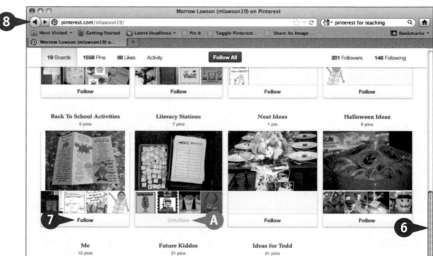

TIP

I understand and enjoy following teachers' boards, but how do I engage students?
Children and teens love the visual feel of Pinterest. You can ask students to comment on pins you post on topics of interest or invite them to contribute to a group board you create. Those actions require that the students be Pinterest members. If you, they, or their parents are not comfortable with that option, you still can use your Pinterest boards as writing prompts and to store references for your students, among other possibilities.

Organize a Wedding

You can get endless great ideas at Pinterest for planning a wedding. After all, wedding pins are among the most popular at Pinterest. Pinterest makes lots of sense for wedding planning when the bride is in Los Angeles and the parents are in Albuquerque. You can create a group board if you want bridesmaids to pin dresses that they like — or you can pin bridesmaids dresses that *you* like and ask the bridesmaids to comment. If you want to be discreet, however, you might keep your real name off your account and make sure your pins do not publish to Facebook.

Create a Set of Boards

Create boards for key areas where you are seeking ideas for the wedding. Possible boards include bridal dresses, wedding cakes, invitations, photography ideas or photographers, flowers, and reception. Once you have created the boards, start pinning or repinning images you see as you view the Wedding and Events category on Pinterest and as you scan such wedding websites as www.theknot.com, www.marthastewartweddings.com, or www.brides.com. If you are on a tight budget, do not be discouraged by all the expensive items you see. Search on Pinterest using terms such as *DIY wedding* or *budget wedding*. You will discover you are far from alone in having a modest affair.

Invite Your Co-Planners

Be sure to invite your fellow wedding planners or advisers to join Pinterest. Once they join, make sure they are following you, and you may want to give them tips on how to check in with your pins. Give them your profile URL, which displays your boards by default. Your URL is http://pinterest.com/*username*/, where *username* is your Pinterest username. If your co-planners are already Pinterest members, ask them to follow you or at least your wedding boards. If they are enthusiastic pinners, you can invite them as collaborators on all or some of your wedding boards so that they can add pins. Or, you can ask them to create their own board of ideas for your wedding.

Notify Your Helpers of Your Pins

Some of your co-planners will be better than others about keeping up with your pins. Take advantage of the Pinterest notification option, especially when you want to make sure that, say, the maid of honor sees the bridesmaid's dress you just pinned. To do so, add an alert in the description by typing @ and then the maid of honor's name as it appears on Pinterest. Pinterest helps by displaying names of people you follow as you enter letters. Once you click **Pin It**, Pinterest not only adds the pin to your board, but it also sends an e-mail notification to the maid of honor.

Refine Your Options

As you get close to making your decisions, create a couple of additional boards. Call them Option 1 and Option 2, or something more clever. Repin to them the images of the combinations that you are considering. For example, on each combination board, include one choice for dress, hair, bridesmaids' dresses, attire for groom and groomsmen, bride's bouquet, and other flowers. Repinning them from your boards keeps them on your original board, such as your wedding dress board, as well as on the options board. Also, repinning lets you easily use one item on multiple options boards.

perfect for that extra tube of lipstick and the iPhone for photos...LOL

1 repin

Solicit Feedback

Set deadlines for key decisions. About two weeks before you need to decide, ask your co-planners to review your options boards and to comment on their favorite dresses, themes, flowers, or whatever you want their opinions on. Give them a deadline for commenting a few days ahead of your decision deadline. Ask them to say why they favor one item or another, which can help you with your decision more than a simple like. Of course, you also may consider the comments and likes of people you do not know who may comment too.

Make and Share Your Decisions

After you have made your decisions, it is time to create a board where you pin your choices. You may want to delete your options boards so as to eliminate confusion. However, keep your original idea boards so that you have backup if something you chose for your final plan does not work out. A fun idea for your decisions board is to create a *save the date* pin showing your wedding date. Then, set that pin as your final plan's board cover. If you are still pinning after the honeymoon, you could do a comparison board showing how it really was!

mint colored dresses!

Use Pinterest for Your Gift Registry

You can make life easier for yourself and for the people who may buy you gifts by using Pinterest along with www.myregistry.com to register your gift wishes. MyRegistry has two tools, a browser add-on and an import feature that lets you add items from Pinterest to your gift register. MyRegistry, a sort of one-stop gift register, retrieves prices from original pins. Your gift-givers then can look at your register and buy through MyRegistry, which keeps track of purchases. You can use it as a bridal or baby shower gift register, or as your personal wish list. You can even make it private.

Use Pinterest for Your Gift Registry

1 Go to **www.myregistry.com/ pinterestaddon** in your browser.

2 Scroll to the bottom of the page.

3 Type your e-mail address.

4 Type a password.

5 Click the **Type of Registry** down arrow ([▼]) and select a registry type from the drop-down list.

6 Click **Create Registry**.

The screen changes.

7 Type the result of the equation in the box.

8 Click the **Terms of Sale Agreement** option to accept the site's terms (☐ changes to ☑).

9 Click **Create Registry**.

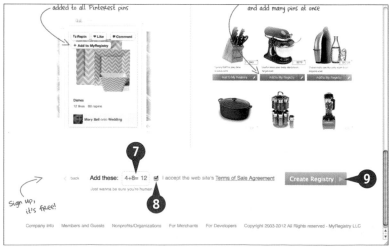

MyRegistry sends you an e-mail message, and the Pinterest tools page opens.

⑩ Click **Get the Add-On for Pinterest**.

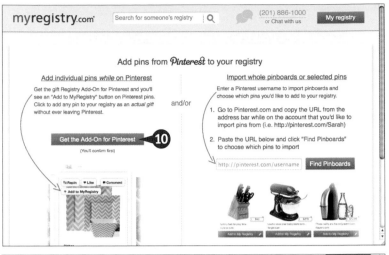

The add-on for the browser you are using opens in a new tab.

⑪ Click the **Add to** *your browser* button; in this case, **Add to Firefox**.

Ⓐ At this writing, Firefox had not verified the add-on, so a warning appears when you click.

⑫ Click **Add to Firefox**.

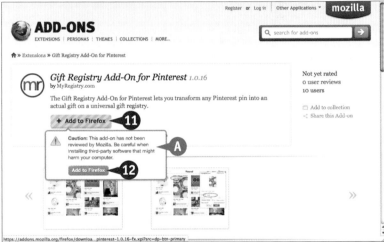

An install dialog box appears.

⑬ Click **Install Now**.

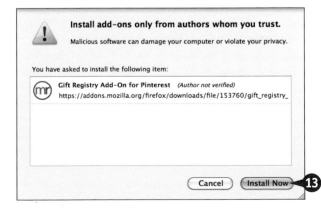

continued ▶

Once you sign up at MyRegistry, its tools make quick work of creating a gift list from your Pinterest pins. The Pin to MyRegistry button appears whenever you position the mouse pointer over a pin at Pinterest. A click of the button opens a dialog box where you can add the item to your registry. Also, you can review Pinterest boards — yours or other members' boards — while at MyRegistry. Then, you can add items you see to your registry with a click.

Use Pinterest for Your Gift Registry (continued)

A dialog box appears.

14 Click **Restart Now**.

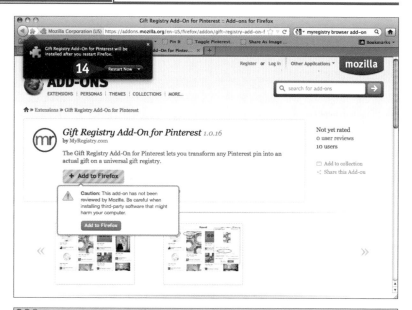

Firefox restarts and returns to the add-ons page.

15 In the address box, type **pinterest.com** and press
Enter .

Pinterest opens to the home page.

🔟6️⃣ Position the mouse 🔺 over an item.

The Add to MyRegistry button appears.

1️⃣7️⃣ Click **Add to MyRegistry**.

The MyRegistry dialog box appears.

1️⃣8️⃣ Click **Add!**

Note: A price and quantity are required.

The add-on adds your item to your list at www.myregistry.com, and the Success! dialog box appears.

Note: It does *not* repin the image to your board.

1️⃣9️⃣ Click the **Close** button (⊗) to close the Success! dialog box.

2️⃣0️⃣ Click the **Add pins...** tab.

continued ▶

If you are viewing the pin through boards at www.myregistry.com, and you click such an item, a pop-up window provides instructions on how to find the source and the price. It requires that you install a bookmarklet to add the item, when you find it, to your registry. If you use the Add to MyRegistry button at Pinterest, you can type in a price, and the button will add the item to your registry. However, shoppers may then be surprised when they click the gift item and discover that the price is incorrect.

Use Pinterest for Your Gift Registry (continued)

The MyRegistry Pinterest page becomes active.

21 Type your Pinterest profile URL.

22 Click **Find Pinboards**.

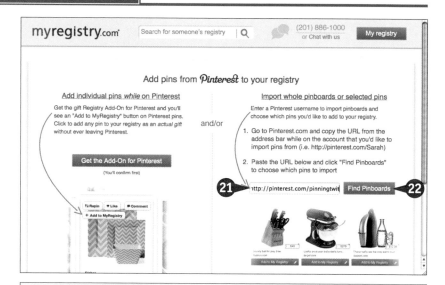

A list of boards appears.

23 Click **Select Pins** next to a board from which you want to register gifts.

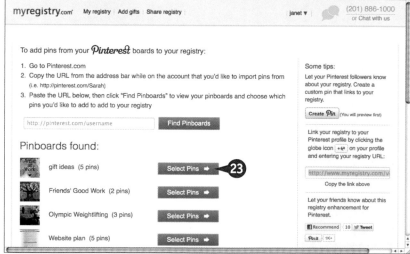

Ⓐ Pins from the board appear.

㉔ Click **Add to My Registry** under an item.

Ⓑ The item is added to your registry and the button changes to Gift Added!.

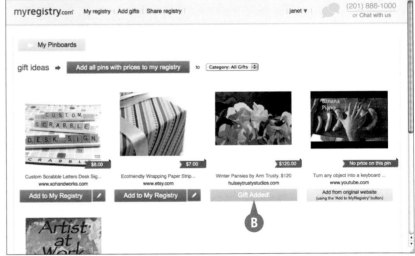

TIPS

Do I need to do anything with the e-mail that MyRegistry sends me?

You do not need to right away. The message asks that you complete your signup at MyRegistry. Doing so involves providing your name, address, and phone number. You also can specify a requirement that visitors need a password to view your register. If you do not complete the signup, you still can add items to your register, but your list is not visible to others.

How do I make my register private?

After you have logged in, click the Actions & Preferences button near the top of the page. A pane appears with various preference check boxes. Click the **Make Registry Private and Not Searchable** check box option. Your register is now available only to you.

Pin Your Portfolio

If you have a professional portfolio or need one, you can post it at Pinterest. Your portfolio needs to contain whatever you would include in a paper portfolio — samples of your best work, your business card or equivalent, testimonials if possible. Your Pinterest portfolio needs to link to your website, and vice versa. Although Pinterest clearly lends itself to portfolios for artists, graphic designers, and photographers, other freelancers can create a Pinterest portfolio too. Start by giving your profile page a professional look, and then create a set of boards that highlights your portfolio work.

Pin Your Portfolio

1 While logged in to Pinterest, click your name, and select **Settings** in the drop-down list.

The Edit Settings page appears.

2 Scroll down to the About section.

3 Type your professional description, including a phone number.

4 Type an address.

5 Type your website URL, including **http://**.

6 Scroll to the bottom of the page.

7 Click **Save Profile**.

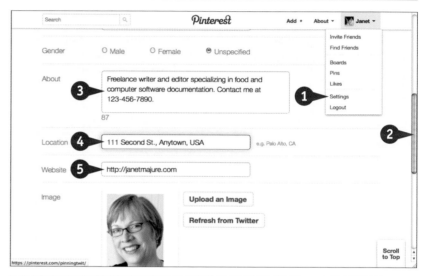

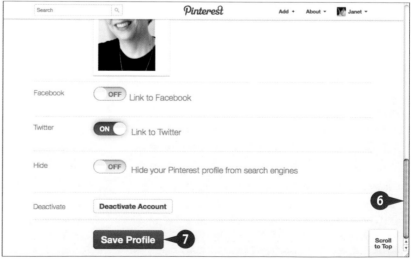

Pinterest saves your profile changes and returns to the profile page.

8 Click **Add+**.

The Add dialog box appears.

9 Click **Create a Board**.

The Create a Board dialog box opens.

10 Type a board name.

Note: Choose a name that reflects the desired content for one section of your portfolio.

11 Click the **Board Category** ▾ and select a category from the drop-down list.

12 Click **Create Board**.

Pinterest opens the board's page, which at this point contains no pins.

13 Repeat Steps **8** to **12** until you have a board for each section of your portfolio, and then pin content to the boards.

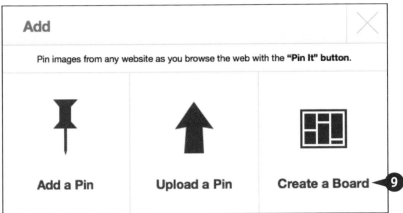

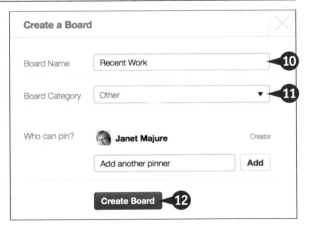

TIP

What else can I do to make my portfolio worthwhile?
Make sure all images in your portfolio link to the place where the photo, painting, or article appears on the web. Use words in your portfolio board titles that can help people find you, such as *Professional Photography Portfolio*. Include links on your website, LinkedIn profile, and Facebook page to your portfolio. Make your portfolio somewhat personal, which people like, by posting a good image of yourself as your profile picture. You may want to add a watermark to the photos or art that you created so that you can be sure your credit follows any repins, regardless if the link gets lost.

Post Your Resume

You can get great exposure for your resume when you post it at Pinterest. Of course, if your resume is a page or two of typescript, you have a bit of work to do before it is ready for Pinterest. Still, Pinterest offers an excellent way to demonstrate your creativity, exposes you to many people you do not know exist who may be looking for you, and is one more way to get your name and credentials out in a tough job market. It is too early to know how successful Pinterest is for job-seekers, but it is worth a try.

It Must Be a Picture

The first hurdle for many people is turning their resume into an image. Pinterest allows you to pin image files only, not word-processing files or PDFs. If you want to use your basic resume, you can convert it to an image, although probably not a pretty one, by making a *screen capture* of your resume and saving it as a JPEG or PNG file. Another even less-pretty option is to use a scanner and scan a paper version as a JPEG. To create a screen capture, open your document full screen, press `Print scrn`, then open a paint program and press `Ctrl`+`V`, and save the screen as a JPEG. (On a Mac, press `⌘`+`Shift`+`3`, and the screen is saved to your desktop as a PNG file.)

Create a Visual Resume

If you want to go further than turning your standard resume into a pinnable image, you can create an infographic as your resume. If you are a graphic designer, a visual resume communicates your design skills. If you are not a designer, you still have options. The website http://vizualize.me is all about turning your resume into a graphic. It requires registration. Two websites, www.wordle.net and www.tagzedo.com, create *word clouds* — that is, graphic representations of words with the most frequent or most important words appearing larger than other words. You could use one for your board cover.

Think of the Board as a Unit

Even if you have minimal graphic skills and do not care to hire or learn them, you still can post a resume to good effect on Pinterest. Plan to make a resume board, not just a single pin. Choose an image that really stands out as your cover image. For example, it could be a photo of you on the job or a sticky-note image from Pinstamatic saying "Jill Jones's Resume" or some other message. You can then pin a text-based resume and similar pins so that the board catches the eye. Remember, if someone clicks on a pin, the board to which it is pinned also appears in the pin window.

Create a Resume in Pictures

Another approach is to create a pictorial resume, making sure that you make contact information available somewhere on your board. First, create a resume board. Then, pin images that tell your story and use the descriptions for each pin to clarify. For example, post a good photograph from your college's website, and put in the description something on the order of *Josh Burns, B.A. in mathematics, University of Iowa*. Add images that relate to your skills, and name them in the description. Add images of former employers, and list what you did at the company. If you have received awards, pin them, too.

The George Washington - MBA Class of 2012

Promote Your Resume

Once you have a resume on Pinterest, let friends, relatives, and potential employers know it is there. Include the URL to your resume board in your e-mails and paper resume. Add it to your website, Facebook page, and LinkedIn profile. Conversely, make sure the links associated with your resume pins go somewhere useful. You could have a text-type resume link to your website or LinkedIn profile. If you have a pin for your school, you could link to that university's main page or, better, to the department you graduated from.

More Ideas

Do not think of your Pinterest resume as a one-time effort. Once you have a resume board, add to it. You might pin multiple resumes — one overall resume, one for your project-management work, and one for programming. If you take a class to learn a new skill, post a pin related to the class. Each time you pin something, remember, it appears in your followers' feeds. Ask them to repin your resume. Search at Pinterest to see other pinners' resumes, or find good examples at http://pinterest.com/pinterestresume/resumes or http://pinterest.com/adrienne/reference-cvs.

Integrate Snapguide Tutorials with Pinterest

If you use the fun and easy iOS app called Snapguide to create tutorials, you can pin your tutorials to Pinterest at the same time you publish them to Snapguide. When you tap Publish after creating your Snapguide tutorial, you can choose to share your creation at Pinterest. Snapguide then presents screens for you to use when creating your pin. When you are done, Snapguide posts your tutorial on its website, and a pin on your Pinterest board shows one image from your tutorial and a caption consisting of your tutorial's title and your name.

Integrate Snapguide Tutorials with Pinterest

1 In Snapguide on your iOS device, tap **Publish** when you have finished your Snapguide tutorial.

A sharing screen appears.

2 Tap **Pinterest**.

The screen displays all the images in your tutorial.

3 Tap a representative image to appear on Pinterest.

The Add A Pin screen appears.

4 Tap the **Board** arrow (▷).

5 Tap a board.

A check mark appears next to the board, and the screen automatically returns to the Add a Pin screen.

6 Tap **Pin It**.

The app publishes the tutorial to Snapguide, pins the image to Pinterest, and returns to the Sharing screen.

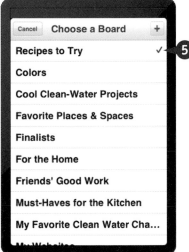

TIP

How can I make it clear on Pinterest that my guide is a tutorial?
You can include the word *tutorial* in your guide's title when you create it at Snapguide. Another option is to edit the description at Pinterest to make it clear that the pin links to a tutorial. For example, the description could say *Step-by-step guide to making baby food*.

CHAPTER 10

Protecting Yourself

Pinterest poses a variety of protection issues, and you can find ways to address most of them. Those issues include spam, copyright questions, spoof pinners, and more. As a social-networking website with record-setting growth, however, Pinterest has not satisfied everyone who has complaints.

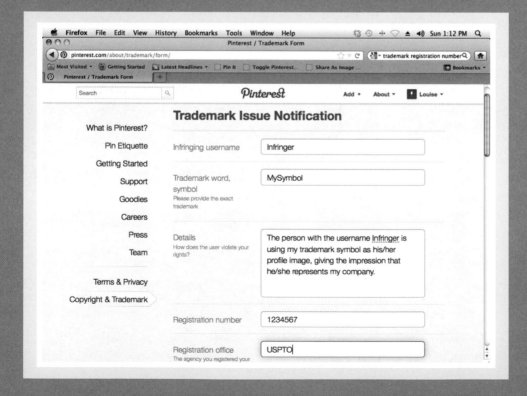

Review Your Pinterest Settings

You can review your Pinterest sharing settings to find out what connections you have authorized. You may be content to leave them as they are, but it is useful to know what your settings are and what they may mean for you. To find out what those settings are, you need to click your name at the top of a Pinterest page, and then select Settings in the drop-down list. Your Edit Profile page opens, where you can see what your settings are.

Ⓐ Link to Facebook

Current status, *in this case On,* for linking to Facebook. This connection allows you to log in to Pinterest with your Facebook information and to find Facebook friends on Pinterest.

Ⓑ Add Pinterest to Facebook Timeline

Current status, *in this case On*, for your pins to appear in your Facebook Timeline. Link to Facebook must be set to On for the timeline option to be available.

Ⓒ Link to Twitter

Current status, *in this case On,* for linking to Twitter. This connection allows you to log in to Pinterest with your Twitter information and to notify your Twitter followers of your pins.

Ⓓ Hide Your Pinterest Profile

Current status, *in this case On,* for hiding your Pinterest profile from search engines. *On* means your profile is hidden; *Off* means search engines can find it. Changes in this setting may take a week or two to affect search results.

Unlink Your Twitter Account

You can easily unlink your Twitter account from your Pinterest account. You can do it even if you used Twitter as your means of signing up at Pinterest. Once you are signed up, though, you are free to sever the connection. It is a matter of changing the settings for your Pinterest account. Once you do, you cannot sign in to Pinterest by way of Twitter unless you agree to re-create the connection.

Unlink Your Twitter Account

1 Click your name at the top of a Pinterest page, and select **Settings** from the drop-down list.

The Edit Profile page opens.

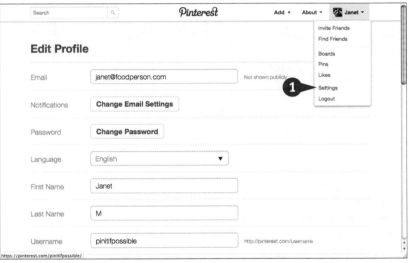

2 Scroll down to the Twitter area.

3 Click the **Link to Twitter On** button to turn your connection Off.

The toggle changes to Off.

4 Click **Save Profile**.

Pinterest saves the changes and opens your profile page.

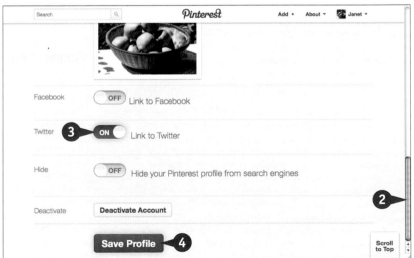

221

Change Your Pinterest Settings at Facebook

You can keep your Pinterest and Facebook connection while limiting what appears on Facebook and who can see your Pinterest pins. Of course, your pins remain entirely public at Pinterest, but by reviewing your Facebook settings, you can decide who sees your pins and other Pinterest activity. You need to go to your Timeline view at Facebook and make your way to the Pinterest activity page. Once there, you can see and change who sees your Pinterest activity and what activity they see.

Change Your Pinterest Settings at Facebook

1 On your Facebook page in the Timeline view, click the **Timeline** menu.

2 Click **Pinterest**.

The Pinterest view opens.

3 Click **Activity Log**.

The Pinterest Activity Log opens.

4 Click the **Audience Selector** menu and select **Friends** from the drop-down list.

5 Click the **Action** menu ( ) and select click any item where you do not want activity to appear.

Note: All items are selected by default, meaning activity appears in those locations.

6 Click anywhere on the screen to close the menu.

7 Click your name.

Facebook returns to your Timeline page.

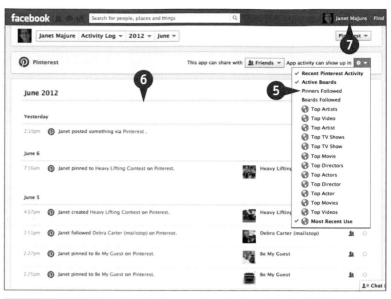

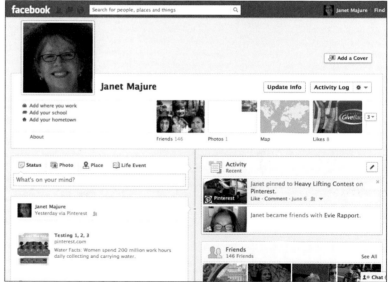

TIP

How can I tell what my friends or others are actually seeing of my Pinterest pins at Facebook?
Click the **Action** menu ( ) next to the Activity Log on the Timeline page, and select **View As** from the drop-down list. Facebook displays your profile page as it appears to the public. Near the top is a box that reads *Enter a friend's name*. In that box, type a Facebook friend's name and press Enter . Facebook displays your timeline as it appears to your friend. If your Pinterest settings include a subset of your friends, you can try names of people in subsets and names of regular friends to see what each sees.

Unlink Your Facebook Account

Y ou can sever the Pinterest link to Facebook completely or in part. Simply go to your Pinterest Edit Profile page, make the desired changes, save them, and you are done. You can choose to end sharing your pins on Facebook, or you can end the relationship entirely. You can take these actions, even if you used Facebook as your means of joining Pinterest. If you unlink entirely from Facebook, however, you will be unable to sign in to Pinterest by using Facebook.

Unlink Your Facebook Account

Stop Link to Timeline

1 Click your name at the top of a Pinterest page, and select **Settings** from the drop-down list.

The Edit Profile page opens.

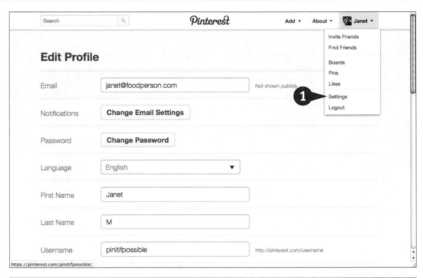

2 Scroll down to the Facebook area.

3 Click the **Add Pinterest to Facebook Timeline On** button to turn your connection Off.

The toggle changes to Off.

End All Facebook Connections

4 Click the **Login with Facebook On** button.

A dialog box appears.

5 Type your Pinterest password.

6 Click **Disconnect Facebook**.

A The toggle changes to Off, and the Timeline connection option disappears.

7 Click **Save Profile**.

Pinterest saves your changes and opens your profile page.

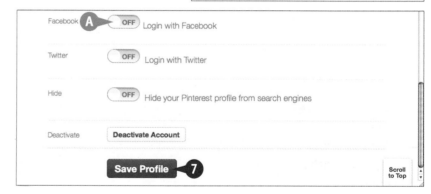

TIP

What do I do if I change my mind and want to connect to Facebook?
You need to return to the **Edit Profile** page, where you click the **Login with Facebook** toggle. Doing so prompts a dialog box to open. You need to reaffirm your permission for Pinterest to connect with Facebook. Then you can log into Pinterest using Facebook, and your pins appear in your Facebook Timeline.

Report Spam Pins

You can help arrest Pinterest spam by reporting dubious pins when you happen across them. In a likely scenario, you click an image you like and go to the pin page. On the pin page, you click the image, but instead of going to the image's source page, you are invited to complete a survey. At that point, you need to click the browser's Back button to return to the pin, and then click the Report Pin button.

Report Spam Pins

1 On the pin page of the suspicious pin, click **Report Pin**.

The Report Pin dialog box appears.

2 Click the **Spam** option (⭘ changes to ⦿).

3 Click **Report Pin**.

A Report Pin confirmation appears.

④ Click the **X**.

Report Pin ④

Thanks for reporting this pin! Our team will review the pin and delete it if it violates the **Pinterest Terms of Use**.

The confirmation disappears, and the pin window reappears.

Maple Kee
Pinned 1 day ago from justgirlthings.com
Follow

Like 0
Tweet
Embed
Report Pin
Email

2394275677831/flag/

TIPS

How can I tell if a pin has already been reported?

There is no way to tell, so it is a good idea to go ahead and report any suspicious pin. Sometimes, a pin that Pinterest has identified as spam still appears on someone's board. When you click it, however, Pinterest displays a message letting you know.

Sorry!
We've blocked this link because it may go to spam or other inappropriate content.
Back to Pinterest · More Info

What does Pinterest do when I report a pin?

The company says it investigates the pin and the account from which the pin was made. It can take days, however, for Pinterest to take action. In addition, Pinterest may block suspicious pinners from further activity on the site until they have been cleared as legitimate.

Identify Fake Pinners

You can help deter the spread of spam when you identify and shun fake pinners. It is a good idea to check out a pinner before you repin his or her pin, even if it slows your pinning. Fake pinners tend to share a few traits. Among them is a tendency to follow many pinners. They often have more boards than they have pins, and many boards are empty. Some link to inactive Twitter accounts. Once you have identified a fake pinner, do not repin his pins and thereby spread the spam. Also, you can report the pinner to Pinterest.

Identify Fake Pinners

A Many more boards than pins on pinner's profile raise suspicions.

1 Click a board.

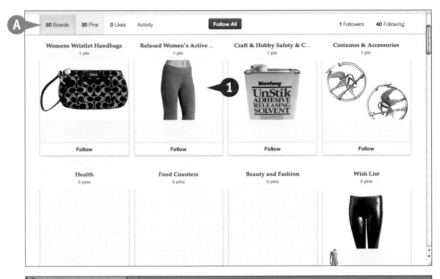

The board opens.

2 Click the image.

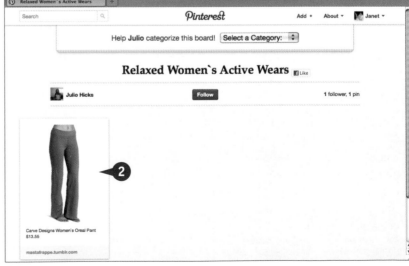

The Pin page opens.

3 Click the image.

The pin's source opens.

B A button requiring action raises suspicion.

4 Click the **X** to close the scam site.

Note: In this example, the button links to a sales page at Amazon.

TIPS

Should I do anything about the fake pinner who is following me?
You can send Pinterest a report on a pin from that pinner as possible spam. You can also make sure that you do not follow the pinner. You cannot block that pinner or any pinner from following you, however.

Should I worry about a pin of a beautiful image with a description that is totally unrelated to it?
It probably is a good idea to assume that the image is spam or that the pinner is a spammer. Tools exist that allow scammers to create numerous accounts, pins, comments, likes, and so on, and goofs such as inappropriate descriptions can tip you off.

Submit a Spammer Report

You can go a step further in reporting a scammer if you do not feel that reporting a pin is enough. To do so, you can submit a request to the Pinterest support staff. You need to copy the URL of the suspected spammer. Then, go to the Pinterest Submit a request screen, select a topic to help direct the request to the right place at Pinterest, and include the URL in your request. The support section displays articles you can read about spam when you select Spam/Abuse as your request topic.

Submit a Spammer Report

1 Click in the address field and Press **Ctrl**+**C** to copy the URL of the profile you want to report.

2 Type **https://support.pinterest.com/home** in your browser.

3 Click **Submit a request**.

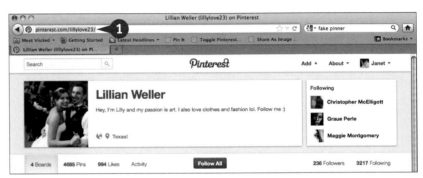

4 Type your e-mail address.

5 Click **None** and then select **Spam/Abuse**.

6 Click **Report User**.

7 Click **Spam or Advertising**.

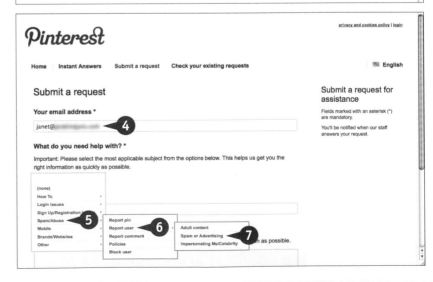

8 Scroll down to complete the report.

9 Type a subject.

10 Type a description, and paste the URL of the pinner.

11 Click **Submit**.

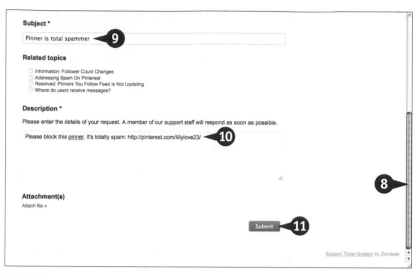

Pinterest opens your requests page, which notifies you that your request has been created and says Pinterest Replied. It also sends you an e-mail.

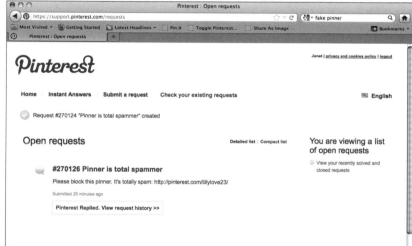

Change Your Password

You can protect the integrity of your Pinterest account by changing your password periodically. Experts recommend changing it at least once every 90 days. Whenever you do, make sure you follow good password practices by using a combination of uppercase and lowercase letters plus numbers and symbols. Also, avoid easily deciphered passwords such as your address and famously common passwords such as *password*. To change your password, you need to go to the Edit Profile page, type in your new password, and save the settings.

Change Your Password

1 Click your name at the top of a Pinterest page, and select **Settings** from the drop-down list.

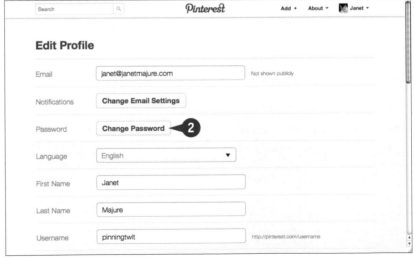

The Edit Profile page opens.

2 Click **Change Password**.

The Change Password page opens.

3 Type your current password.

4 Type a new password.

5 Retype the new password.

6 Click **Change Password**.

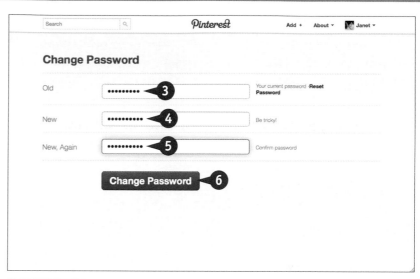

Pinterest saves your password and returns you to your profile page.

TIP

What are the Pinterest requirements for passwords?

Unlike many websites, Pinterest at this time does not have any specific rules for what you include in your password. You therefore bear all responsibility for coming up with a password that is easy for you to remember but hard for others to guess. Besides using a combination of uppercase and lowercase letters, also include numbers and symbols. One example might be a favorite song title and the last two digits of your phone number, *HEIotS#83*, for *His Eye Is on the Sparrow* plus number, or #, and *83* for the last two digits of your phone number.

Give Credit to Image Creators

You can reduce the odds of legal issues if you give proper credit when you pin or repin images. Doing so is easy when you create a new pin. However, repinning may require extra steps. Do not repin from a feed. Click the image to see the pin page, and then click the image to see its source. If the source is questionable, you may want to reconsider the repin, or create a new pin from the original source, if you can find it. Always avoid repinning images that show thousands of repins, even if all repins are legitimate.

Give Credit to Image Creators

1 Before repinning, click the pin image to see the source.

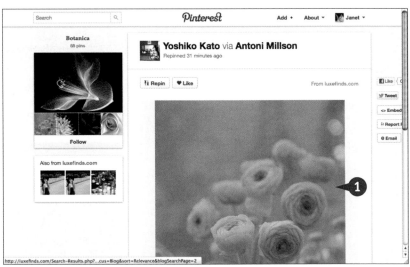

The link opens in a new tab. In this example, the source has used an image from another site.

A The web page title implies its purpose does not involve the image subject.

2 Click the link to the image source.

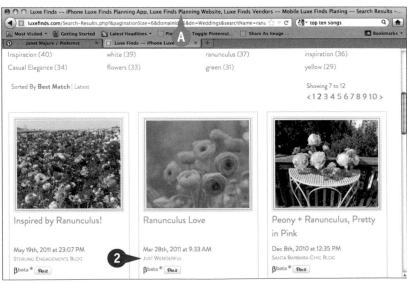

The link opens in a new tab. In this example, the source has used an image from yet another site.

3 Click the link to the image source.

What seems to be the original image source appears.

4 Click **Pin It** to initiate a new pin from the original image.

TIPS

How can I give credit when I am pinning?

To give credit when you are pinning, in the Create Pin dialog box, click the **Board** down arrow ▾ and then select a board from the drop-down list. Type a description that includes the website name or the URL for the article with the image or both. Click **Pin It**. In the Success dialog box, click **See your Pin**. Pinterest automatically includes the source.

How does giving credit protect me?

By giving the original source credit, it shows you are complying with the Pinterest Terms of Service. Also, it tells creators that you acknowledge their work. Still, until all legal issues are resolved, the only *guarantee* against being blamed for misusing images is to pin your own material, those in the public domain, and those with licenses permitting reuse when properly attributed.

Block Pin It Use at Your Website

Yyou can prevent Pinterest members from using the Pin It bookmarklet to pin images from your website. You can do it with a bit of code that Pinterest introduced in response to complaints from people who did not want their pictures reproduced at Pinterest. The code also has variations. One allows you to bar pinning of specific images, rather than blocking pinning across your entire site. The other lets you create a custom message for people who try to pin from your site. These options block pinning only from the bookmarklet, the most common pinning method.

Block Pin It Use at Your Website

Block Bookmarklet Sitewide

① In a code editor, type **<meta name="pinterest" content="nopin" />** after the opening <head> tag and before the closing</head> tag.

Note: The <head> tag probably appears in your site's header file, such as header.php.

This example uses WordPress.

② Click **Update File** to save the change.

③ In your browser, go to your site.

④ Click **Pin It**.

Ⓐ A dialog box appears telling you that pinning is not allowed.

⑤ Click **OK**.

The dialog box closes, and the site page reappears.

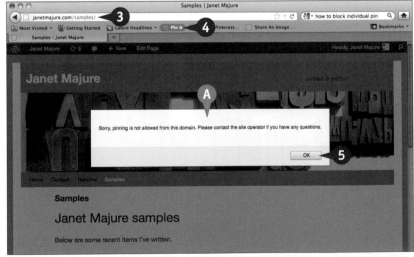

Block Bookmarklet to an Image

1 In a code editor, find the statement starting `<img` associated with the image you do not want to make available to the bookmarklet. Insert the nopin attribute by typing **nopin = "nopin"** before the statement's closing `/>`.

2 Click **Update** to save the change.

3 In your browser, go to the page with the image you are blocking.

A The image displays with nopin code.

4 Click **Pin It**.

Images to pin appear, but the image you blocked is absent.

5 Click **Cancel** to close the Pin It picker.

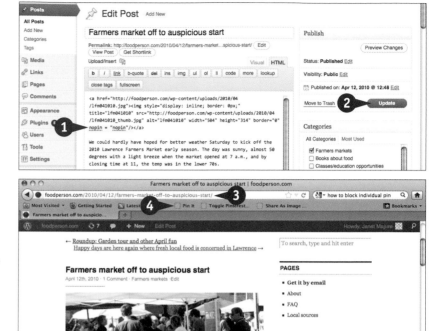

TIPS

How do I customize the text in the no-pinning dialog box?

To do so, add a description to the meta tag. Simply type **description ="Your message"** where *Your message* represents your custom message. When the dialog box appears, the text then reads, *Pinning is not allowed from this page. Yoursite.com provided the following reason:* Your message.

How do people get around the blocks?

They can copy the URL of the page with the image and paste it into the URL box when they click Add+ at Pinterest. Pinterest proceeds with creating a pin. Also, the Pinterest Right-Click browser add-on works even with the code in place. Other means may be available also.

Block Pins from Your Flickr Account

You can block most pins from your Flickr account simply by changing an account setting there. After you change the setting, you still can pin from your Flickr photostream but others cannot, except by taking extra steps, such as copying the URL and using the Pin + link at Pinterest. One nice thing, though, is that using Pin + and adding the URL embeds your information into the pin. Thus, even if someone edits the pin link to show a different URL, your Flickr name and the original Flickr URL still appear under the image on its pin page.

Block Pins from Your Flickr Account

1 In your browser, go to **www.flickr.com/account/privacy**.

2 Click **edit** next to the Allow others to share your stuff option.

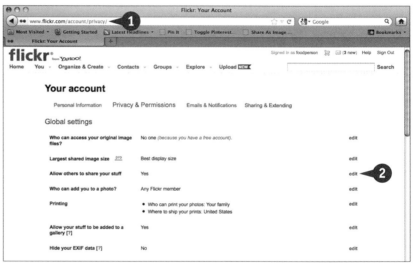

3 Click the **No, thanks** option (○ changes to ⊙).

4 Click **Save**.

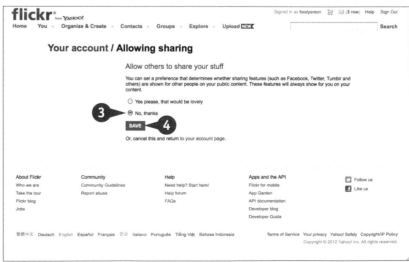

Flickr returns to your account privacy page.

A Flickr confirms the change.

B The Allow others to share your stuff option changes to No.

5 Click **You**.

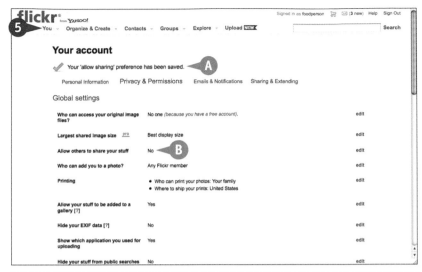

Your photostream opens.

6 Click an image in your photostream.

7 Click **Share**.

C The Share dialog box opens, showing the buttons are dimmed.

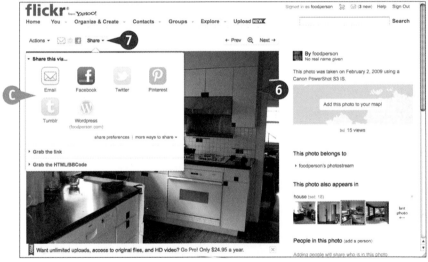

TIP

Why does the Share dialog box still provide a URL, and what can I do to stop pinning this way?
Perhaps the hope is that by providing the URL, a determined pinner will copy and paste the URL at Pinterest. Doing so retains a link to the image's original location on Flickr and your Flickr username, even if the pinner edits the link available in the Edit Pin screen. To entirely block pins from Flickr requires that you close viewing of your photos to everyone except friends and family whom you trust not to pin from your stream.

Report Copyright Infringement

You can ask Pinterest to remove images you own that you do not want pinned at Pinterest. Pinterest provides a form that makes reporting infringement easy. It created the form and a relatively understandable copyright information page in response to complaints from copyright holders. Some people think it is smart to go beyond the form and to also send a notice vie e-mail or postal mail as described on the Pinterest copyright page so that you have better records of submitting your report.

Report Copyright Infringement

1 On the Pinterest page where the offending image appears, click in the Address Bar and press `Ctrl`+`C` to copy the URL.

2 In your browser, go to **http://pinterest.com/ about/copyright**.

The Pinterest copyright page opens.

3 Read the copyright information.

4 Click **Copyright Complaint Form**.

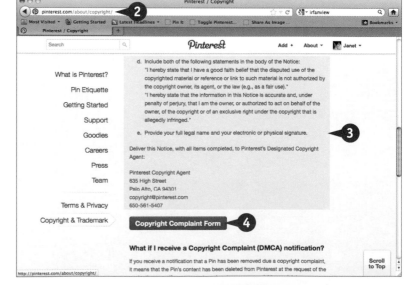

The Copyright Infringement Notification page opens.

5 Type the complete URL of your web page where the image appears.

6 Press Ctrl+P to paste the URL you copied from the offending pin.

7 Type your full name.

8 Type your street address.

9 Scroll down and type the remaining contact information requested.

10 Click to affirm you did not give permission to use the image (☐ changes to ☑).

11 Click to affirm you own or represent the person who owns rights to the image (☐ changes to ☑).

12 Click to affirm the accuracy of your information (☐ changes to ☑).

13 Type your name.

14 Click **Submit Notification**.

Pinterest confirms your submission and lists a request code.

15 Press Ctrl+P (⌘+P) to print the confirmation.

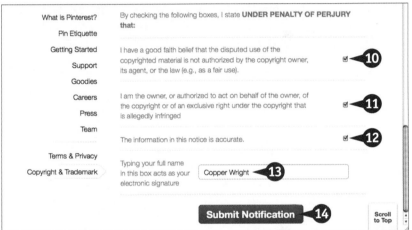

TIPS

Can I instead just use the Report Pin button on the pin page?

That button just provides another route to doing the same thing. If you click **Report Pin** and then click the **Is this your intellectual property?** link, Pinterest opens the copyright page. The button does not record the pin URL, so you still need to copy the URL from the pin window and paste it in the form.

Should I follow the instructions for mailing my complaint instead?

The Digital Millennium Copyright Act of 1998, which you can read at www.copyright.gov/legislation/dmca.pdf, provides specific instructions for written notice. If you have questions, you should talk to an intellectual property attorney.

File a Trademark Complaint

You can use an online form to notify Pinterest if you think someone is using your trademark or service mark in a way you do not want. These issues arise often on the Internet, such as when someone registers a username of a well-known company and poses as a representative of the company. The trademark form requires you to include your trademark registration number. Providing additional information about the registration may help your case. Also, be prepared to choose whether you want to claim the username or blacklist the username.

File a Trademark Complaint

1 In your browser, go to **http://pinterest.com/about/trademark/form**.

2 Type the username of the user you are complaining about.

Note: To find the username, go to the user's profile page, and view the URL. It is in the form http://pinterest.com/*username*/. The username may differ from the name displayed on the page.

3 Type the exact trademark word or symbol description.

4 Type a description of the infringement.

5 Type the registration number.

6 Type the agency with which you registered the trademark.

7 Scroll down to the contact information area.

8 Type your full name.

9 Type your relationship to the trademark older.

10 Type your contact information.

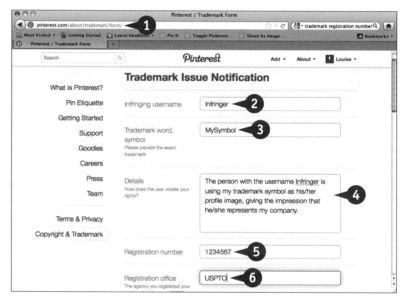

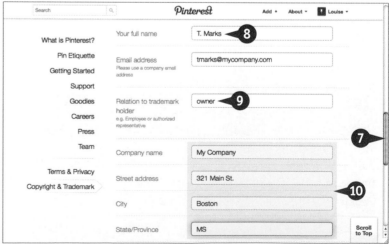

11 Click the option next to the outcome you seek (○ changes to ⊙).

12 Click to affirm you have not authorized the use and believe it violates your rights (□ changes to ☑).

13 Click to affirm the accuracy of your information (□ changes to ☑).

14 Click **Submit**.

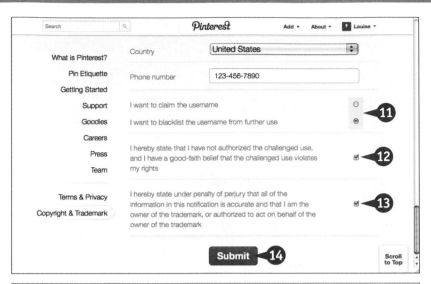

Pinterest confirms your submission and lists a complaint ID.

15 Press Ctrl+P (⌘+P) to print the confirmation.

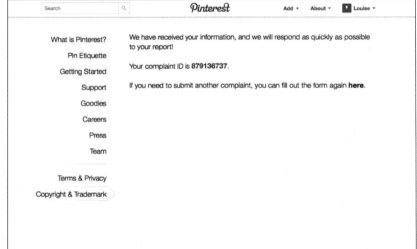

TIPS

Why should I go through Pinterest rather than contacting the infringing party directly?
The primary reason is that you probably cannot positively identify the person using your trademarks. Pinterest may be able to do so. Even if it cannot identify the culprit, Pinterest can shut down the account if it finds that the party is abusing your trademark.

When will Pinterest respond to my request?
It is hard to predict. At this writing Pinterest has not taken action against members whose usernames duplicate names of famous companies. If you doubt it, take a look at http://pinterest.com/generalmotors or http://pinterest.com/pepsi.

CHAPTER 11

Getting Help

While Pinterest is fairly simple to use, it does not provide the world's best help. However, its support pages do answer a limited number of questions, which you can search or browse. You also can submit a support request and find information about Pinterest from a variety of sources.

Get Support on Pinterest

Y ou can get some support on Pinterest, although it may not be as much as you need. Still, it is the place to start when problems arise. You can view the basic help information via the About menu's Help option. From there, you can click Support for more answers to more questions. On the support pages, you get detailed answers to many questions, and can see the issues other Pinterest users have raised that Pinterest staffers are addressing. While you may not find your answer, at least you will know Pinterest is addressing the topic.

Get Support on Pinterest

① Position your mouse ▶ over the About button, and click **Help**.

The Help page opens.

② Scroll down to look for the question you have.

③ Click a question.

Ⓐ The answer appears beneath it.

Note: The answer remains visible until you click the question again.

④ Click **Support** if you do not see your question.

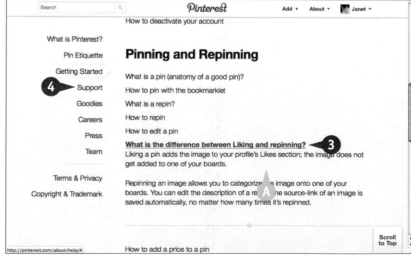

The Support page opens.

5 Type your question.

6 Click **Search**.

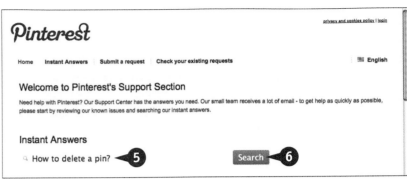

B The page displays related questions.

7 Click a question.

C Pinterest displays the question and answer.

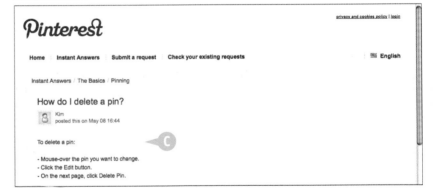

TIP

What are Known Issues, which are listed at the bottom of the support page?

Known Issues are problems that multiple Pinterest members have reported to the Pinterest Support Center. They also are difficulties that site developers are aware of but have not yet corrected. If you see an issue that relates to a problem you are having, click the issue title, which links to more information. Occasionally, that added information may include a form for you to complete if you have the same problem.

Known Issues

Issue: Pin Images Not Loading

Aaron Jun 12 • The Basics / Known Issues

Browse Pinterest Support

You can often find answers to questions by browsing the questions that Pinterest Support posts on its site. This approach may work best if you find you are not very good at coming up with good search terms. Also, as you browse the support questions, you may see answers you were not seeking but are pleased to have. Unfortunately, Pinterest does not have a support forum where you can seek answers from other users.

Browse Pinterest Support

1 In your browser, go to **https://support.pinterest.com/forums**.

2 Click a category.

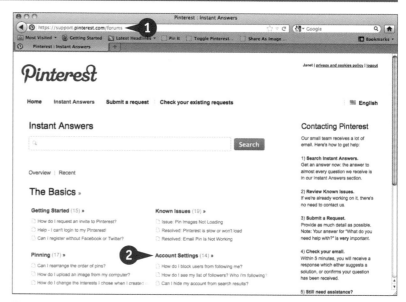

The Instant Answers for the category opens.

Note: The questions appear in the order of most to least useful, based on user ratings.

3 Click a question.

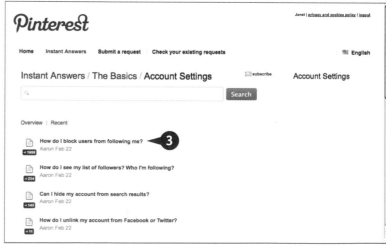

The window changes and shows the question and answer.

4 Click **Instant Answers**.

The Instant Answers page returns.

5 Repeat Steps **1** to **4** as needed.

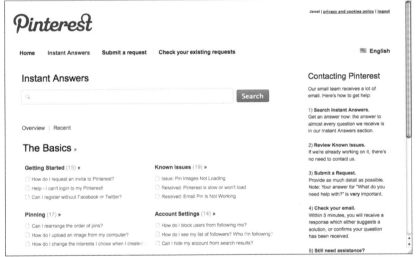

How do I vote for the answers I think are useful?

At the bottom of each answer screen is a statement, *N people found this useful*, where *N* is the number of people. To add your endorsement, click **Me too!** which adds your Pinterest login to the support pages.

The link changes to a thumbs-up button. Click the button. The line changes to read *Your vote has been registered, thanks! (undo)*. You can click **undo** if you change your mind.

Review Known Issues

Y ou can get some relief to Pinterest frustration when you review answers to Known Issues and read recent support entries. Partly because of the rapid growth in Pinterest, the site occasionally runs slowly or does not behave as expected. Also, the Pinterest support pages have not entirely kept up with the surge in members. The Support pages let you check out the latest problems and occasionally get answers. You even can subscribe to get updates on some issues.

Review Known Issues

1 In your browser, go to **https://support.pinterest.com/forums**.

2 Click **Known Issues**.

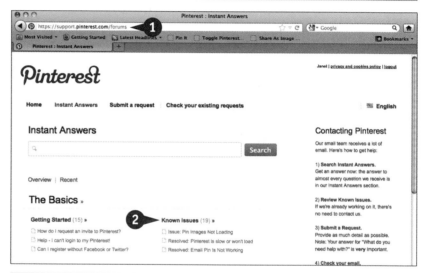

The Known Issues list appears.

3 Click an issue.

The issue page appears.

4 Read the information.

A In this case, a form provides a means to add a report.

5 Click **subscribe** to receive e-mail updates on the issue.

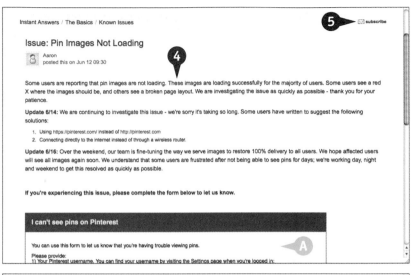

B Pinterest confirms your subscription.

C You can click the unsubscribe button if you change your mind.

6 Click **Known Issues.**

You may repeat Steps **3** to **5** as needed to review issues.

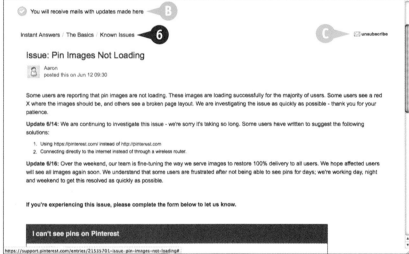

https://support.pinterest.com/entries/21535701-issue-pin-images-not-loading#

TIPS

How can I keep up with all the issues without going to the support pages regularly?
Complete Steps **1** and **2** of this section. Click the **subscribe** link that appears next to the Known Issues title. Pinterest confirms your subscription to all updates of known issues.

Instant Answers / The Basics / **Known Issues** ☑ subscribe

🔍   Search

How can I see the latest changes to support answers?
When you are at https://support. pinterest.com/forums, click **Recent** under the Search box. The view changes to display answers that have changed, with the most recently changed items at the top of the list.

Submit a Support Request

If you cannot find the answer you are seeking by using the Pinterest Support pages, you can submit a support request. Response times can be slow. Pinterest encourages users to check the Support pages' Instant Answers and Known Issues before submitting a request so as to minimize the number of requests. If you decide you need to submit a request, you can start on the Support pages or simply type in the URL for making a request. You need to be signed in at Pinterest. Pinterest confirms your request online and by e-mail. Usually, you need to respond to the confirmation to keep the request active.

Submit a Support Request

1 In your browser, go to **https://support.pinterest.com/requests/new**.

2 Click the down arrow ([▾]) and select a topic.

Note: You must choose a topic.

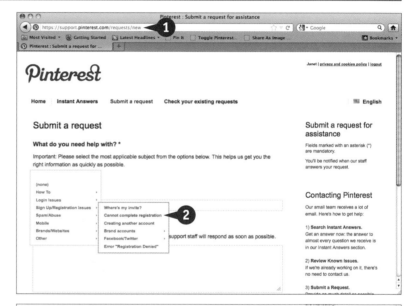

3 Type a subject.

Ⓐ Links to related support answers appear.

4 Type a description.

5 Click **Submit**.

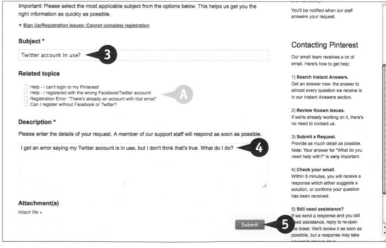

Pinterest opens your requests page and sends you an e-mail.

Ⓑ Status of request.

❻ Click **View request history**.

Pinterest opens the request page.

❼ Scroll down to the comments area.

Ⓒ The text of the e-mail Pinterest sent appears.

❽ Type a response.

Note: If you do not respond, you probably will not hear further from Pinterest.

❾ Click **Submit**.

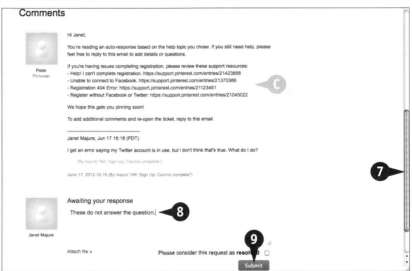

Pinterest returns to the existing requests page.

Ⓓ A message confirms your change.

How can I cancel a request?
Go to **https://support.pinterest.com/requests**, and repeat Steps **6** to **8**. Under the comment area, click the **Please consider this request as resolved** option (☐ changes to ☑). Then click **Submit**. Pinterest returns to the existing requests screen, and a message confirms the change. The request is gone from the Open Requests list.

I did not mark a request as resolved, but it is not in the Open Requests list. Where did it go?
Most requests trigger automated responses. If you do not respond in a day or two, Pinterest moves them to a separate page. Click **View Your Recently Solved and Closed Requests** on the Existing Requests page to see the closed requests. You cannot reopen a closed request.

Report Objectionable Pins

You can report pins that offend you or that you feel violate the Pinterest Acceptable Use Policy. To do so, you need to click through from the feed to the individual pin window. There, you can find the Report Pin button. It opens a dialog box where you can specify the reason for your report. In addition to the standard reasons is the Other option. If you click it, a box appears where you can type your objection to the pin. Once you report the pin, the Report Pin option no longer appears.

Report Objectionable Pins

1 Click **Report Pin**.

The Report Pin dialog box opens.

2 Click a reason why you are reporting a pin (○ changes to ◉).

3 Click **Report Pin**.

The Report Pin box changes and then disappears.

The pin window reappears.

A The Report Pin button has disappeared.

TIPS

Does Pinterest let me know if it deletes the pin I objected to?

It does not. If you want to know, you can repin the pin to a board, or you can copy and save the pin page URL and then check back later. If the pin has been deleted, you will most likely get a 404 error message telling you that the page cannot be found.

Why does Pinterest forbid nudity or pins promoting anorexia but allows images of unnaturally thin women in skimpy clothes?

Only the Pinterest powers can answer that question, although it could be that it is easier to define nudity or pro anorexia pins than it is unnaturally skinny or skimpy ones. You could submit a request to Pinterest Support in the Spam/Abuse > Policies category.

Find Source of Image with Google

You can get help finding the source of an image by taking advantage of Google Search by image. The easiest way to do it is simply to drag the image from one browser window to the Google image search window, and results appear in a flash. Other methods involve pasting the URL of the image or saving the image to your computer and uploading it to the Google image search. You may not always find what you are seeking, but you often will, and it is as speedy a method as you are going to find.

Find Source of Image with Google

1 In your browser, go to **http://images.google.com**.

2 In a separate browser window, open the pin image you want to investigate.

3 Click the pin image and drag it toward the Google browser window.

4 When the Search by image box appears, release the mouse button.

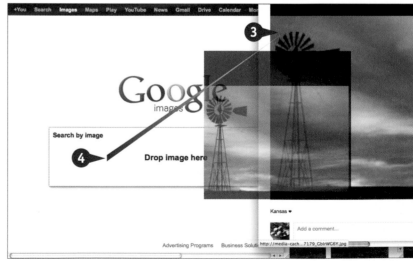

Google opens a page of search results.

5 Click in the Google window to make it active.

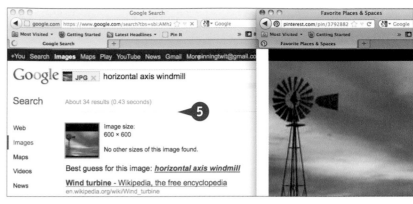

6 Scroll through results.

7 Click the link to a likely source.

The web page with the image appears.

A The original image for this example — with a watermark that someone cropped away later — and a story about the photographer.

TIP

How do I search by image with a URL or uploaded photo?
In your browser, go to **http://images.google.com**, and click the **Camera** icon (📷) in the search box. Paste the URL of a photo, and click **Search**. You need the URL of the actual image, not the web page it is on. Usually, you can get the URL by right-clicking the image and selecting **Copy Image Location**, although this option does not work at Pinterest. Instead, right-click a Pinterest image and select **Save Image As** to save it to your computer. Then, click **Upload an Image** at Google image search, find the image on your computer, click it, and then click **Open** to upload it.

Change Language at Pinterest

You can choose to view Pinterest in languages besides English. Go to your settings page, select your preference from the Language drop-down list, and save your settings. Changing the language setting changes the language in all the text that Pinterest serves, such as menus. It does not translate text that you have entered, such as board names or pin descriptions. It also does not change the language on the support pages. You can change it for these pages separately.

Change Language at Pinterest

1 In your browser, go to **https://pinterest.com/ settings**.

2 Click the **Language** down arrow ([▾]) and select **Espanol (America)**.

Note: This example uses American Spanish. Use the same method for choosing one of the other languages.

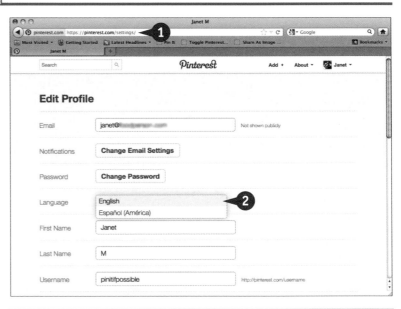

3 Scroll to bottom of page.

4 Click **Save Profile**.

Your profile page opens.

Ⓐ Pinterest-provided text appears in Spanish.

5 Click **Pinterest**.

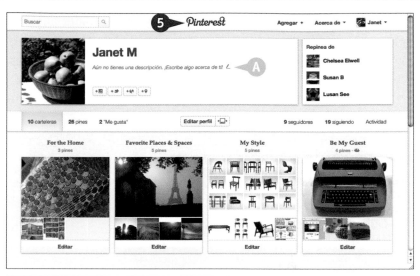

The main Pinterest page opens.

Ⓑ Titles are in Spanish.

6 Click **Categorias**.

Ⓒ The Pinterest categories are in Spanish.

Ⓓ User-added content is in English unless the user typed it in Spanish.

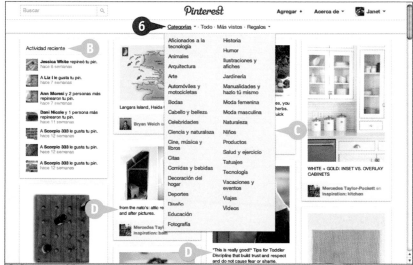

TIPS

How do I change language on the support pages?

Go to **https://support.pinterest.com/home**. Click **English** near the top of the screen and select another language from the drop-down list. The support pages now appear in the language you chose.

How can I see Pinterest in a language besides English or Spanish?

Pinterest has announced that it is translating its service into more languages. At this time English, Spanish, Brazilian Portuguese, Dutch, and German are the only options. As an interim measure, you can try the Google Chrome translation feature. To learn more, go to **http://support.google.com/chrome** and type **translation** in the search box.

Keep Up with Pinterest News

You can get the most out of Pinterest if you keep up with Pinterest news. The methods you choose to keep track of news depend on the type of information you want and on how much time you have to sort through it. The possibilities include getting messages from Pinterest, following Pinterest-related boards, and checking out Pinterest-themed websites. Each approach has its appeal and drawbacks, but you can find one that works well for you.

Receive E-Mails from Pinterest

Pinterest offers a variety of e-mail notifications. To make sure you get them, go to **http://pinterest.com/ prefs**. Click the on-off toggle on each setting to meet your preference. Most of them pertain to notifications when people pin, repin, or follow you. Two different options appear at the bottom of the page. You can get

an e-mail message updating you on what you have done on Pinterest, and you can choose to get news updates from Pinterest. Make sure the News toggle is set to On. Then, click **Save Settings**. Also, go to **http://support. pinterest.com/forums**. Click the **Known Issues** category, and click **Subscribe** at the top of the Known Issues list.

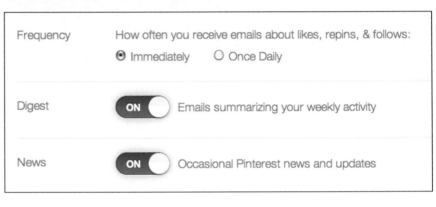

Follow Pinterest-Related Boards or Pinners

Numerous Pinterest members have pinboards where they record Pinterest news. When you follow them, their pins show up in your feed. Among the good boards to follow is the infographic-laden Pinterest News board at http://pinterest.com/mobileholly/ pinterest-news. The News on Pinterest board at http://pinterest.com/jivay/news-on-pinterest links to news articles on new media websites as well as on the web pages of print magazines. The pinner Pinterest for Business, at http://pinterest.com/pinterestbiz, has numerous Pinterest boards of interest not only to people wanting to use Pinterest for business but also for anyone keeping up with general Pinterest topics. It also provides links to websites focused on Pinterest.

Create a Google Alert for Pinterest

Y ou can get daily e-mail messages with links to the newest Pinterest information on the Internet. It is easy with the help of a Google alert. To create a Google alert, you go to the appropriate Google page, provide your e-mail address, and make some decisions as to the alert content. After you confirm your desire to get the alert, Google starts sending you e-mail roundups of new web content that focuses on Pinterest. You can click links in the alerts to see to the full web article in your browser.

Create a Google Alert for Pinterest

① In your browser, go to **www.google.com/alerts**.

② Type P**interest** in the Search query box.

③ Click the **How often** down arrow (▾) and select your frequency preference.

④ Type your e-mail address.

⑤ Click **Create Alert**.

The screen changes, confirms your alert, and advises you to click the link in the e-mail verification that Google sends you.

⑥ Go to your e-mail account and locate the verification e-mail.

⑦ Open the email and click the verification link to confirm your request.

The Google verification window opens. Alerts begin at once on the schedule you chose.

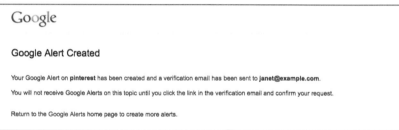

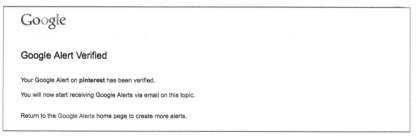

Reactivate Your Account

If you receive a notice that Pinterest has deactivated your account, you can contact Pinterest support to get back in business. The notice usually gives a reason for the deactivation. It may be the result of someone submitting a report about a pin, or it could be that the Pinterest computers mistakenly identified you as a source of spam or other violation of Pinterest rules. Your pins and boards are still available. Pinterest says it responds to reactivation requests within a day.

Reactivate Your Account

1 In your browser, go to **https://support.pinterest.com/requests/new**.

2 Click the down arrow (▾) and select **Login Issues**.

3 Click **Reactivate**.

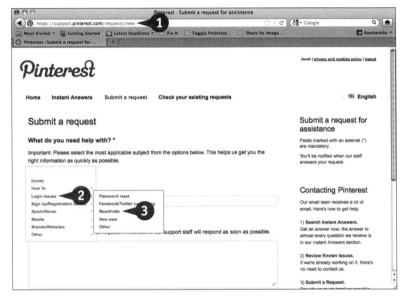

4 Type **Reactivate account** in the subject box.

A A list of support articles appears.

5 Type **Reactivate account**.

6 Click **Submit**.

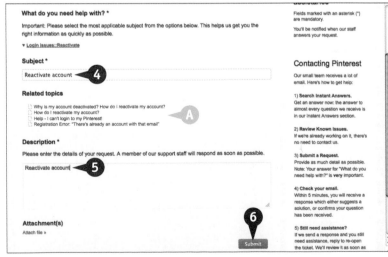

Pinterest sends you an e-mail and opens the Open requests screen.

7 Click **View request history**.

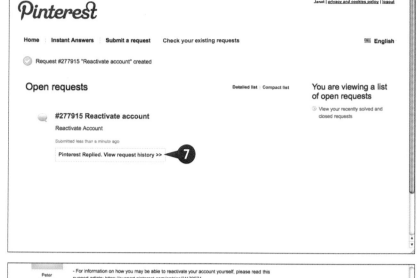

Details of your request appear with information on how to reactivate your account.

8 If you are still unable to reactivate your account, scroll down to Awaiting your response.

9 Type **Still need help**.

10 Click **Submit**.

Pinterest updates your request and sends an e-mail notifying you that your ticket has been reopened.

TIP

What can I do to keep from getting deactivated in the first place?
You can make sure that you pin, repin, like, and comment at a moderate pace. In an effort to arrest spam, Pinterest computers watch for excess activity from individual accounts. If you get a message from Pinterest telling you to slow down, or if your attempt to repin an image does not seem to work, do proceed at a slower pace.

Deactivate Your Pinterest Account

You can deactivate your Pinterest account if you decide you do not want to use it. Perhaps you have not been active on the account and do not like the idea of it being on display without your participation. If you deactivate your account, Pinterest stores your pins and boards. If you later change your mind, you simply log back in to Pinterest, and your account becomes active again. If you want to remove the content of your account, you can do so separately but Pinterest cannot restore it.

Deactivate Your Pinterest Account

1 In your browser, go to **http://pinterest.com/ settings**.

2 Scroll to the bottom of the page.

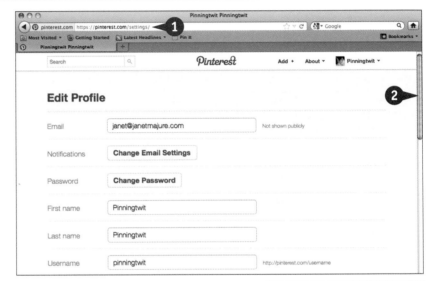

3 Click **Deactivate Account**.

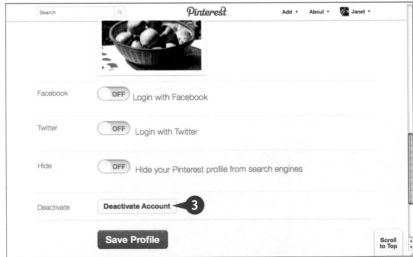

A Deactivate message appears.

4 Scroll down to see the entire message.

5 Click the **Yes, I want to deactivate my account** option (☐ changes to ☑).

6 Click **Deactivate My Account**.

A deactivation message appears for a moment.

The Pinterest home page appears, and you are no longer logged in.

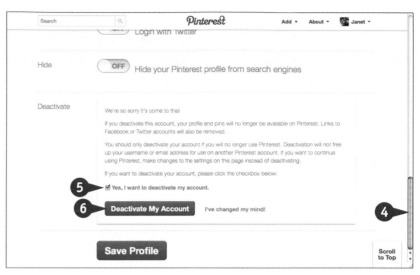

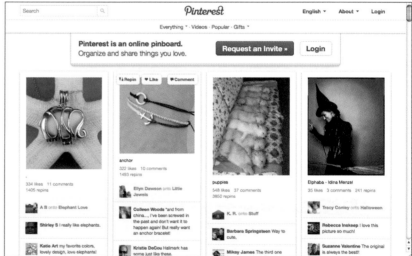

How do I totally eliminate my Pinterest pins if deactivating my account does not?
The easiest way is to delete your boards before you deactivate the account. You cannot undo such actions. If you have many boards, it may take a little while to do. To delete a board, you need to open the board, click **Edit Board**, click **Delete Board**, and then confirm the deletion in the dialog box that appears. The board and the pins on it are gone forever.

Index

Special Characters and Numerics

C

Want instruction in other topics?

Check out these
All designed for visual learners—just like you!

978-0-470-94219-2

978-0-470-50386-7

978-1-118-15173-0

e Available in print and e-book formats.

For a complete listing of *Teach Yourself VISUALLY*™ titles and other Visual books, go to wiley.com/go/visual